Ready for Prime Time
Devotions for Girls

By Andrea Stephens

Beautifully Created
Stressed-Out but Hangin' Tough
Prime Time: Devotions for Girls
Ready for Prime Time: Devotions for Girls

By Bill and Andrea Stephens

Prime Time: Devotions for Guys
Ready for Prime Time: Devotions for Guys

Ready for Prime Time
Devotions for Girls

Andrea Stephens

Fleming H. Revell
A Division of Baker Book House
Grand Rapids, Michigan 49516

Material on pages 59–61 is adapted from *Beautifully Created* by Andrea Stephens.

Material on pages 20–31, 107–08, and 113–15, is adapted from *Stressed-Out but Hangin' Tough* by Andrea Stephens, © 1989 by Andrea Stephens. Used by permission of Fleming H. Revell Company.

Library of Congress Cataloging-in-Publication Data

Stephens, Andrea
    Ready for prime time : devotions for girls / Andrea Stephens.
       p. cm.
    Summary: A collection of devotional readings for teenage girls, examining such topics as spiritual strength, self-acceptance, prayer, and stress.
    ISBN 0-8007-5459-X
    1. Teenage girls—Prayer-books and devotions—English. 2. Teenage girls—Religious life—Juvenile literature. 3. Devotional calendars—Juvenile literature. [1. Prayer books and devotions. 2. Christian life.] I. Stephens, Andrea. II. Title.
    BV4860.S75   1993
    242'.633--dc20   92-31717

Published by Fleming H. Revell,
a division of Baker Book House
P. O. Box 6287, Grand Rapids, Michigan 49516-6287

Printed in the United States of America

To all the special young women who are striving to be Christian examples in today's crazy teenage world. My heart and prayers are with you. Be strong. You can do it!

Partners in Christ,

Andrea

A heartfelt thanks to:

My guest authors and special friends, Barbra, Karen, Lenne Jo, Carolyn, and Judy. I appreciate your willingness to share your guidance with these young ladies!

My youth group girls at Covington Presbyterian Church, who read parts of this manuscript, as well as Barbra, Francie, Bill, and Carol.

My friend Carol Mulker, who once again joyfully typed this manuscript, taking a heavy load off my shoulders!

And to my caring family and friends for their much needed prayer support!

Contents

A Word from the Author

Hey! Check This Out Before You Get Started!

Congratulations! Whether you have already completed my first devotional, *Prime Time,* or you are just starting your devotional journey, I'm so proud of you! Spending time with God every day is the most important thing you can do for yourself!

I know your life gets rushed and absolutely filled to the brim. Piles of homework, student council meetings, cheerleading practice, boys, piano lessons, swim meets, youth group, boys, tennis tournaments, drama club rehearsal, band practice, your new job, television, and boys! There are so many things pulling you in different directions, competing for your time. And there are only twenty-four hours in each day! Girls are busy, busy, busy!

Plus, in this teenage time of life, when you are struggling to figure out who you are, it seems everyone has an opinion about everything! Your parents say one thing, your friends say another, your social life is pulling you in one direction, your church in another, some of the music you listen to says to forget God and just please yourself. So many voices! Who are you supposed to listen to? Who can you believe?

That's why more than ever before, you need to set aside some Prime Time with God! Spending time learning from God's Word and having heart-to-heart prayer time with Jesus will give you the guidance, wisdom, and strength you need to make it in the nineties. So, I wrote this book to help you. I've included the important stuff you need to know.

Here's How to Use It

Pick a time five or six days each week when you are awake and alert to do a short study. I suggest trying to study at the same time each day—before school, after dinner. Don't do it late at night on your bed when you're ready to fall asleep. Chances are you won't remember a thing the next day!

Each week you will study one topic. Begin each day with prayer, asking God to open your heart and mind to his truth. Now, dig in! Look up the Scriptures. Write your responses. Ask yourself how you can start living out what you're learning. Then, close each day with the suggested prayer, including other needs you want to tell God about. Listen intently for God's answers. Watch closely for his hand working in your life.

At the end of the week, review the Scriptures you read each day and pick out your favorite one. Now write it out in the space provided. Challenge yourself to memorize it. Hide it away in your heart. You can do it!

If you start to fall behind in your study, don't quit! Just pick up where you left off or start fresh with a new week. Do your best and be flexible.

You may find it helpful to share this devotional book with a sister or a girl friend. It can be used for individual or small group study. I recommend that you use a

New American Standard or The Living Bible to accompany this book.

I pray these devotionals will change your life. It wasn't until I started studying God's Word for myself that I was able to really get my life on the right path. My life took on a whole new meaning. I hope these studies will do the same for you. Enjoy your Prime Time with the Lord!

Your friend,

Andrea Stephens

Supernatural Strength

Guest Author: Karen J. Sandvig

God Power

Be still, and know that I am God.

Psalm 46:10 NIV

It was almost time to leave for the basketball tournament. Jen was a bundle of nerves. She paced back and forth in front of her bedroom mirror, trying to think of last-minute reasons why she might stay home. She could say she was sick.

No, she couldn't do that to her coach or teammates. On the other hand, if her anxiety grew much worse, she really would be sick and have to bow out of the state championship games.

Jen's mother, Sally, said from the doorway, "Honey, it's almost time to go."

Jen turned around and wailed, "Oh, Mom! I'm such a mess! I'm scared to death to go out on the floor tonight! What if I blow the game? What if I make a fool of myself—or the whole team?"

Sally walked into the room and sat on the edge of the bed. She said calmly, "Jen, try to hold on to *God's* power instead of your own. If you can be still long enough to let him be God, things will work out just fine no matter which team wins or loses the game! God's power gives you the strength to do your natural best, and then to deal with *whatever* happens."

Please, Father, help me in times of anxiety and fear to let my heart be still and remember that you are God.

Prime Time This Week

When life gets crazed, out of wack, or throws you a curve ball, you may too often forget to turn to God. How foolish! He's the very One who can pump you back up and give you courage and confidence. He is the almighty God! His strength in you will see you through! Find out how this week.

Monday 12/26/94

Many teens turn to friends, television, music-blasting Walkmans, food, alcohol, cigarettes, and so on when life gets rough. They grope for anything to hang on to that might make them feel better. God says "STOP! Look only to me." Read Isaiah 41:10. What have you turned to instead of God? What happens when you do? How is turning to God so much better? _When I get in a nerveous sisitiou I usually turn to my friend, but If I turn to god he will help me with the problem but_

Prime Prayer: Ask Jesus to help you focus only on him when life gets tough, knowing he holds the answers in his hand.

my friend is only giving me the chance to get it off my chest or mind.

Tuesday 12/27/94

As Christians, what powerhouse are we to plug into to get our strength? Find it in Philippians 4:13! How has God given you strength in your life? What was the situation? Do you need more power to help you through a tough situation right now? Write out a prayer explaining your problem to Jesus and asking him to fill you with his strength. God my problem is when ever my brother comes home it brings out the worst in me, so please help me show my good sides as much as possible.

Wednesday 12/28/94

Power is perfected in weakness! Read Paul's story in 2 Corinthians 12:7–10. When you recognize your weakness and your dependence on God, then his power can work through you. What are your areas of weakness? Are you depending on the Lord? _____

_____

_____

_____

Prime Prayer: Ask the Lord to help you stop trying to do everything on your own and to rely on his power to work through you.

Thursday 12/29/94

Ephesians 6:10–17 tells us to put on the full armor of God so we can be strong in the strength of his might. That's ultimate power! What are the six pieces of God's armor? Describe how each piece can make you strong.

_____

_____

_____

_____

Prime Prayer: Ask Jesus to remind you each day, as you dress for school, to put on the armor of God as well.

Friday 12/30/94

Psalm 46:10 instructs us to be still and to realize that God *is* who he says he is. Being still means sitting quietly, clearing your thoughts, calming your worried, racing mind. Only when you shut down will you be able to hear the Lord speaking to you. What thoughts are pounding loudly in your mind, demanding your attention? Give them over to the Lord and be still! _____

_____

_____

_____

Prime Prayer: Tell the Lord about the things you put in front of him. Then ask him to help you realize he *is* God!

This week's memory verse: Pick it! Write it! Remember it!

_____

_____

_____

_____

Charades

> But let it be the hidden person of the heart, with the imperishable quality of a gentle and quiet spirit, which is precious in the sight of God.
>
> 1 Peter 3:4 NASB

Have you ever felt that others don't really know you? That there's another person deep inside longing to get out, to be known? That's the hidden person of your heart. The real you.

Some girls find their lives are like a game of charades. Either they act loud, boisterous, and rebellious, or they are very shy and withdrawn, scared to let someone get close and know them. Some girls spend their time trying to be what they think their parents or friends want them to be, covering up who they really are. Why? Oftentimes, because their self-esteem has been crushed, they are afraid to just be themselves for fear others won't like them. So, they cover up, play charades. They wear colorful makeup, fancy hairstyles, elaborate clothes and jewelry, and expensive perfume, or maybe they purposefully avoid these things in an effort to hide.

That tactic might work on some people. We usually don't let the quiet and gentle side out because it doesn't get much attention. It's not as aggressive as the world teaches and admires. But God says it is the hidden person of your heart, the real you, that he is looking at. He wants the inner you to be laced with a quiet and gentle spirit. Quiet doesn't mean shy; it means peaceful and restrained, not rebellious and uncontrolled—bossing others around, resenting the authority of adults, refusing to take responsibility for actions.

Gentle, of course, means kind, caring, and considerate—soft, not harsh. When our personalities, words, and actions are quiet and gentle, that is an imperishable—nondecaying—quality that is *precious* in the sight of God. When you act ugly and unbecoming, you are not the young woman God wants you to be. You are not honoring him. What you do and say reveals just how gentle and quiet your inner person is. Maybe you have "quiet" and "gentle" mastered. Maybe you need to take five and evaluate and improve in other areas. As Colossians 3:17 (TLB) says, "And whatever you do or say, let it be as a representative of the Lord." May you always bring glory to him by letting out that hidden person of your heart. No charades needed any longer.

> Dear Lord, am I pretending to be someone that I'm not just to be accepted by others? Help me let the real me shine. May it be a reflection of the quiet and gentle-spirited person you desire me to be. Amen.

Prime Time This Week

Acceptance is a need everyone has. To be liked and loved for who you are helps you to grow and blossom into the person God truly wants you to be. Yet, total and honest acceptance is hard to find. That's why people wear masks. They pretend to be someone they really aren't in hopes of being accepted. If everyone continues to wear a mask, no one will ever really know anyone else. Perhaps you have a mask you need to take off. As you show people who you really are, eventually they will do the same. And it won't really matter if others accept and like everything about you. It's impossible for everyone you meet to like you. We are all different. We can accept others based on their personhood. It's so reassuring to know God doesn't judge us the way others do. His love is a big love. He accepts us into his family with open arms.

Monday

The real you, the inner person, is where God desires truth. Read Psalm 51:6. When you are truthful about who you really are, you are being wise. Who in your life do you need to be yourself with? How do you think they'll respond to the real you? _____

_____

_____

_____

Prime Prayer: Ask God for courage as you start to let others know who you really are, what you think, and what you feel.

Tuesday

Thousands of girls have a poor self-image because they don't feel good enough. They think they're inadequate. What does God say? Read 2 Corinthians 3:4–5. As a Christian, where does your adequacy come from? How can God help you measure up? _____

_____

_____

_____

Prime Prayer: Pray today for God to replace your feelings of inadequacy with his adequacy!

Wednesday

Start today by reading Romans 9:20. What did the clay say to the potter? Have you ever asked God that same question? How does God see you? Read Psalm 139:13–14. How does this help you appreciate your individual uniqueness? _____

_____

_____

_____

Prime Prayer: Ask God to help you see yourself as a one-of-a-kind, irreplaceable treasure because, in his eyes, that *is* what you are!

Thursday

Does your self-image suffer because you don't feel you have a purpose in life? God wants to change that! Read the following verses and record God's purpose for you in each of them: Ephesians 2:10; Colossians 1:10; Matthew 5:16. _____

_____

_____

_____

Prime Prayer: Thank God today for creating you for the purpose of doing good work for others!

Friday

God wants you to be your *best* self! How are you being less than your best? What or who is holding you back? God made you just right. Be yourself! _____

_____

_____

_____

Prime Prayer: Ask God to show you how to be your best for him.

This week's memory verse: Pick it! Write it! Remember it!

_____

_____

_____

_____

_____

Just Between You and the Lord

O Lord, hear me praying; listen to my plea, O God my King, for I will never pray to anyone but you.

Psalm 5:1–2 TLB

"I'm so glad it's Friday," announced Janet, as she flopped onto the sofa after a hard week at school. "I need to have some fun. Mom, can I have Nancy over and rent a movie tonight?"

"Sounds okay," Janet's mom replied. "What movie do you have in mind?"

"Well, after school, Nancy and I wrote down our three favorite videos. Here's the list." Janet airplaned the piece of paper to her mom, who scanned the choices.

"Janet, Dad and I have always said no to this first choice. We don't want you to see it. Why even ask again?"

"Well, Mom, because it's Nancy's favorite movie. Her parents let her watch it. She's probably seen it a dozen times. I swear, everybody I know has seen it. I don't think it sounds so bad." Janet folded her arms defensively. "I can't wait until I'm old enough to watch whatever I want!" she mumbled.

"All right, Janet, tell you what. Let's practice what we heard in church. You go have a few quiet moments with the Lord. If he tells you that movie's all right, then I won't argue."

"Really? You mean that?" Janet asked, dashing off to her room. As she started to pray, she suddenly remembered a song she used to sing:

> Be careful little eyes what you see.
> The Father up above is looking down in love.
> Be careful little eyes what you see.

Janet dragged herself back to the kitchen knowing she had heard from God. "Oh, Mom, you already knew what the Lord would say."

"Janet, someday soon you will be making these choices on your own. You'll no longer be accountable to Dad and me. It'll just be between you and the Lord."

Janet's mom touched her daughter's hand. "Jan, God's not trying to ruin your fun, but he does want to protect you from harm."

"But Mom, it's hard when I feel I'm the only one not allowed to do something."

"I know, honey, but praying, and then doing what God wants will pay off. It'll keep you on the path he has designed for you."

"I suppose," Janet sighed. "Well, I really wanted number two on the list anyway. I guess I've got a good excuse to tell Nancy we're choosing *my* favorite movie!" Janet grinned.

"Oh, yeah, the one you've rented so many times you could have bought your own copy?" her mother laughed. "Let the movie be my treat tonight. How about some popcorn to go with it?" Janet and her mom hurried out the door to pick up Nancy and the movie.

Oh, Father, the more time I spend with you and come to you with my questions, I will know what to do. Help me to be strong. Take away the loneliness I feel when my friends choose things that I know you wouldn't like. Help me to be strong and do what you want me to do. Thank you for reminding me to be careful! Amen.

Prime Time This Week

Prayer is one of the privileges we have as Christians. It is a time when we can go to our heavenly Father and tell him everything that's on our heart. We can also ask him for guidance and wisdom in every situation we face. Yet, prayer is more than a privilege; it's a necessity. It is something we *need* to do. It allows us to spend valuable time in God's presence. We build a deeper and more intimate relationship with him through prayer. It's a time when we can get recharged, renewed, and strengthened to go back out and battle the world. Prayer is also a time when we can learn to surrender our will to the Lord so he can make us willing to accept his perfect answer to our prayers. This week let's see what else we can learn about the privilege and power of prayer.

Monday

When Jesus needed to pray, he went away to a place where he could be alone. Read Matthew 6:5–6. Where can you be alone with God to pray? Of course, you *can* pray anywhere, anytime. In fact, lots of times during the day you'll find it necessary to send quick "pop-up" prayers to God. Who and what can you pray about? What does it say in Philippians 4:6 and Matthew 5:44? _____

_____

_____

_____

Prime Prayer: Ask God to teach you to live in an attitude of prayer, ever ready to come before him with your needs or needs of others.

Tuesday

Some people think they don't have the right to go to God with their needs. Read Ephesians 3:12. It says that because we have Jesus, Christians have _____ and _____ access (to God) through faith in Jesus! How will knowing this help in your prayer time?

_____

_____

_____

_____

Prime Prayer: Pray that you will better understand God's great love for you and his desire for you to come to him with confidence.

Wednesday

A sign posted on a church bulletin board read: "A person who kneels before God can stand up to anything!"

It's so true! How has prayer made you stronger and more confident? (Hint: It helps to remember what you've prayed for and to expectantly wait for God's answer!)

_____

_____

_____

Prime Prayer: Ask God to fill you with strength, courage, and peace as you faithfully make time in your daily schedule to pray.

Thursday

Guess who is praying for *you?* Yes, probably your mom and dad and a friend or two. But who else? Read Hebrews 7:25; Hebrews 9:24; and Romans 8:34. Wow! Jesus makes intercession for us in the presence of God! Intercession is praying to God on behalf of someone else. Jesus prays for you! How does that make you feel? How does it boost your confidence?_____

_____

_____

_____

Prime Prayer: Praise God today for Jesus, who appears before God on your behalf!

Friday

Prayer is not to be taken lightly. Jesus always prayed for knowledge of God's will, for guidance, and for the needs of others. Read Colossians 4:2. What two instructions does this verse give? Now read Colossians 4:3.

Prayer changes things! What was Paul asking God to do? Need changes in your life? Pray! _____

_____

_____

_____

Prime Prayer: Ask God to help you devote yourself to prayer, knowing that prayer does make a difference.

This week's memory verse: Pick it! Write it! Remember it!

_____

_____

_____

_____

_____

Stress!

I'm Stressin'

Thou wilt keep him in perfect peace, whose mind
is stayed on thee: because he trusteth in thee.

Isaiah 26:3 KJV

Stress. It has become so common in the nineties that
it's accepted as a normal part of life. In fact, it's practically fashionable. Stressed-out is the way to be. Or is it?
Do any of these situations sound familiar to you?

It's 7:16 A.M. Sharon was supposed to leave the house
by 7:03 A.M. to catch the school bus. But that was the
least of her worries. She could stand the embarrassment
of being late to first period, but she didn't have her Eng-
lish paper completed. Plus she didn't have a clean uni-
form for gym class and couldn't remember the soccer
rules for the quiz. Besides that, she was sure to run into
Tom, and she hadn't talked to him since their Saturday
night date, which had ended in a fight. Sharon's mind
was racing; her palms were starting to sweat. The knot
in her stomach made her feel like throwing up. Her
mind screamed, *Why do I feel this way?*

Kristie was happy she had landed a new job as a waitress. It would really help out with her car payments. But she was worried. *What if I forget to turn in a food order or spill an entire milkshake in someone's lap? And what if the restaurant is packed? Can I serve all those tables at once?* She just wasn't sure of herself. She felt a headache coming on, and she didn't even have to report to work for two more hours!

Kristie let all the things that could possibly go wrong fill her thoughts. She became stressed-out. And she had two whole hours of worry until it would be time to start work. Her new job was already giving her a headache and nervous body.

Ann was having a hard time at home. Her parents fought constantly, and they rarely talked to her unless, of course, there was something they wanted her to do. She felt alone and isolated. She felt that everything happening around her was out of her control. She was stressed. Ann expressed her need to have control by refusing to eat. At least, that was one thing she could be in charge of. It was also her quiet way of rebelling against her parents. Ann was showing signs of anorexia.

Sharon, Kristie, and Ann are stressed-out! Stress is the feeling you get when you get tense, worried, uptight, and feel you have little control over your life. You long for inner calmness or peace. But how do you get it? The technique that worked in *The Karate Kid* will work for you—FOCUS!

When you are feeling stressed, where do you focus your thoughts? On the problem, or on the Lord? Isaiah 26:3 offers the key to stomping out stress! Focus your thoughts on the Lord and he will give you the peace you need to make it through tough times. School, parents, guys, a job—whatever is stressing you out, hand it over to the Lord. Trust him to work it out for good. Then you will feel his peace gently fill you.

Dear Jesus, when life gets tough—and even when it's not—keep my thoughts on you so the strength of your peace will keep me going. You, Jesus, are the Prince of Peace. Be the prince of my heart. Amen.

Prime Time This Week

The stress you experience in your life usually starts in your head! In your thoughts! Your thoughts can cause or calm your worries. Thoughts can give you ulcers or take them away. Control your thoughts and you'll control your stress. Inner peace and lack of stress are directly linked to your mind, according to Isaiah 26:3. Let's see how you can focus, fix, and glue your thoughts on the Lord so his peace replaces your stress.

Monday

Trust is a vital ingredient in stress reduction. After you pray, do doubtful thoughts and questions still fill your mind? Trust the Lord! Stop worrying! Read Romans 8:28. How does this verse help you to trust the Lord and his plan for your life? _____

_____

_____

_____

Prime Prayer: Ask God to continually remind you that he is in control of your life, working out every detail. He is dependable and can be trusted!

Tuesday

We already know that thoughts affect your stress level. Well, exactly what kind of thoughts are you supposed to have that will lessen stress? Read Philippians 4:8–9. List the things you are to think about. When you think on these things, what does verse 9 promise you will receive in return? _____

_____

_____

_____

Prime Prayer: Ask Jesus to help you keep your thoughts on what is pure, good, positive, and in line with his Word. Now make an honest effort to do it!

Wednesday

Are you afraid God doesn't know what you're thinking about? Do you think he is unaware of your needs? If so, tell him everything! In exchange for your troubles and worries, his peace will guard your _____ and your _____. Find out in Philippians 4:6–7.

Prime Prayer: After you tell God your thoughts, ask him to surround or guard your heart and mind with his peace, keeping doubtful thoughts far away!

Thursday

Don't let negative thoughts enter your mind. Chase them away whenever they try to sneak in. Talk positive to yourself and watch how your stress level goes down, down, down! Write three positive statements about a situation that is troubling you. _____

_____

_____

_____

Prime Prayer: Ask God to help you keep the thoughts that you think in the silence of your mind very positive and very trusting toward him.

Friday

All teens struggle with stress. But stress is just a warning signal that says there is something else going on that you're trying to cope with! That's why I wrote an entire book on the subject! My book *Stressed-Out, but Hanging' Tough* will help you identify and cope with the stress in your life. Get a copy today!

Prime Prayer: Ask the Lord to help you identify the situations in your life that are stressing you out now, and hand them over to him!

This week's memory verse: Pick it! Write it! Remember it!

_____

_____

_____

Hot, Hot, Hot

So because you are lukewarm, and neither hot nor cold, I will spit you out of my mouth.

Revelation 3:16 NASB

Have you ever stopped to think how useless lukewarm water is? Now if it were cold water, it would be great for cooling you off, quenching your thirst, or chilling raw vegetables. And if it were hot water, it would be perfect for relaxing in a bubble bath, cleaning the dishes, or hard boiling an egg.

But lukewarm water can't do any of these things. Lukewarm is sort of like nothingness. It's just stuck in the middle, right between cold and hot.

Let's talk food. How about pizza? I love to eat it hot. I love to eat it cold. But lukewarm? It doesn't taste so good.

The same is true in Jesus' opinion when it comes to some Christians. He calls them lukewarm, meaning they are not completely turned off to God, and yet, they are not completely turned on to him either. They are not hot or cold! They are in between. Indifferent. Sure, they went to camp one summer and accepted Christ, but they don't live a Christian life-style. You won't catch these teens telling their friends about Jesus, or throwing away their Van Halen, Pink Floyd, or Motley Crue tapes. Lukewarm Christians go to Friday night parties, have a few beers, and think nothing of it. And church? Oh yeah, church. Well, an occasional appearance is enough for them. Anything to keep Mom and Dad off their back.

Lukewarm Christians don't taste good to the Lord. The only way to improve their flavor is to get HOT! That's right. Get turned on, be on fire for the Lord—100 percent Christian, 100 percent of the time. Get hot, hot, hot for the Lord!

Lord, forgive me for the times I have been indifferent and lax in my relationship with you. Place your fire in me and lead me to be hot for you. Amen.

Prime Time This Week

This week you'll look at what it means to be hot for the Lord and how to turn your temperature up for him. As with anything in your life, if you approach God half-heartedly, you won't get the full benefit of your relationship with him. Your life may feel empty and meaningless. The choice is yours, but please, DON'T BE A FENCE RIDER! Get hot for Jesus!

Monday

The big dinner with no guests! Read the parable in Luke 14:15–24. These people were indifferent toward God, putting petty things before him. What were their excuses for not attending the dinner? What excuses do you sometimes give for not following the Lord, not accepting his invitation when he calls? _____

_____

_____

_____

Prime Prayer: Ask the Lord to convict you when you are flinging out excuses about not following him. Now repent and start saying *yes* to Jesus.

Tuesday

One key to a hot, sold-out relationship with God is the Holy Spirit. Read Matthew 3:11 and Acts 2:1–4. What do you think the Holy Spirit's fire is, and how does it help you be a "turned on" Christian? _____

_____

_____

_____

Prime Prayer: Ask each day for the Holy Spirit to fill you with his fire and desire!

Wednesday

To be hot for God means to have an uncompromising attitude. Job had this kind of attitude. He continually trusted and obeyed God no matter what his circumstances were or what his friends said. Read Job 1:20–22 and 2:7–10. After Job had endured, what was his reward (found in Job 42:7–17)? _____

_____

_____

_____

Prime Prayer: Ask God to help you withstand the pressure and teasing from others as you choose to be sold out to him! The reward is great!

Thursday

Mary and Martha were sisters and best of friends. But Martha got bothered when Mary left her, and she had to prepare and serve dinner all alone. What did Jesus tell Martha in Luke 10:38–42? Why was Mary's choice better than Martha's worry over dinner? How can listening at Jesus' feet turn you on to the things of God?

_____

_____

_____

_____

Prime Prayer: Ask Jesus to give you the wisdom of Mary— to spend more time learning about him and loving him instead of letting daily duties get you down.

Friday

When you do things that are inconsistent with God's desires for you, your witness for him is weak. Your friends and classmates should be able to see there is something different about you. Are there changes you need to make in your life-style that will allow you to show a clearer picture of your Christianity? What are they? Get started now! _____

_____

_____

_____

Prime Prayer: Ask the Lord to show you changes you need
to make in your life so you can be turned on to serving
him and being a good witness to others.

This week's memory verse: Pick it! Write it! Remember it!

_____

_____

_____

_____

_____

Give Me a Light

Thy word is a lamp to my feet, and a light to my path.

Psalm 119:105 NASB

Have you seen the popular, overplayed Bud Lite commercials on TV? I think anyone who ever watches the tube, even for a few minutes, has seen them. The scene is usually of a burly ole guy demanding a "lite" from a meek-looking, servant-type fellow. So the little guy goes out and brings back a light, any kind of light, just to please the big guy. First he brings a candle, then a torch, then a glass chandelier, then a blinking neon light! But that's not what the big burly guy wanted. He wants a *Bud* Lite. He probably would have gotten what he requested if he'd been more specific. *Lite* and *light* sound the same! But let's give that little guy a break. He was just trying to do his job. He *did* bring a light. A typical light is something that gets rid of the darkness, and he did return each time with that!

Light is very necessary, no matter what the form. Light helps us see where we're going. If we roam around in the dark, we will get lost and probably trip and fall over something. We need light! In Psalm 119:105, God's Word, the Bible, is called a light. God's Word gives us direction and guidance. When you aren't sure what to do in certain situations, go to the Bible. There you will find helpful words of instruction that will filter through your confusion and shine a clear light on the path God wants you to take. Without the light, you will end up on the wrong road or be doing the wrong thing. You will stumble around in the dark. First Peter 1:25 says that God's Word lasts forever; it provides a solid foundation on which to build your life! So, join me as I say, "Give me a light—God's light."

> Dear Father, sometimes life is rough and the world is dark out there. I don't always know what I should do. Help me to remember to turn to your Word so I can clearly see where I'm going. Amen.

Prime Time This Week

This week, discover how God's Word can act as a light that shines on the road God wants you to take. It will help you with tough decisions. Find a Bible concordance that lists Scripture verses according to subject. Then, look up the topic you are struggling with and see what God has to say about it. Now follow his well-lit path. The following examples will help you get started. Helpful hint: Memorizing the order of the books of the Bible will help you find Scriptures faster!

Monday

Your parents have warned you about going to drinking parties, but you promised Tim you'd be there. Let Colossians 3:20 make your decision. What does it say?

_____

_____

_____

_____

Prime Prayer: Ask God to help you honor your parents' guidance and God's Word.

Tuesday

A classmate just told you some hot gossip. You can't wait till you see Karen next period. She'll just cringe when she hears this. But wait. Should you really pass it on? Read 2 Timothy 2:16. According to this verse, what should you do? Why is this the best decision? How does gossip hurt people? _____

_____

_____

_____

Prime Prayer: Ask God to help you keep gossip to yourself, so it stops with you and stops needless hurt to others.

Wednesday

You and a certain girl have never been friends. In fact, because of what has happened in the past, you are enemies. You snub each other all the time. Check out

Matthew 5:43–48. What does Jesus instruct you to do?
How would acting loving and praying for this girl
change your relationship? _____

_____

_____

_____

Prime Prayer: Ask Jesus to give you the willpower and
the maturity to love and care for others no matter what
they say or do to you.

Thursday

Your brother is very sick and needs you to fill in on
his paper route. Getting out of bed at 5:00 A.M. sounds
horrible. Read and apply Philippians 2:4 to the situation. What would God want you to do? _____

_____

_____

_____

Prime Prayer: Ask God to keep you from always putting
your own desires first and to learn to be concerned about
others' needs.

Friday

You are so worried about flunking your math test,
your best friend being mad at you, and your grand-
mother in the hospital, that you aren't even thinking
about the Lord! Look up Philippians 4:6–9. What can
you do and how can God help? _____

_____

_____

_____

Prime Prayer: Ask God to forgive you for forgetting to turn to him the very times when you need him most!

This week's memory verse: Pick it! Write it! Remember it!

_____

_____

_____

_____

_____

Washing Windows

But if we confess our sins to him, he can be depended on to forgive us and to cleanse us from every wrong.

1 John 1:9 TLB

Brenda was excited about her family's move to the East Coast. She finally said good-bye to all her friends. The next day she would be headed to a new town, a new school, new friends, and a new house. Brenda's parents had purchased a house two months ago when her dad first learned of his transfer. Brenda could hardly wait. She was going to have her own room, and she could decorate it any way she wanted. Her mom's description of the new house was beyond Brenda's dreams. A big white house, a porch swing, a swimming pool, a stone fireplace, a game room. And it was only a few blocks from her new school. For two months the house sat waiting for Brenda and her family.

Brenda was a bit disenchanted when they pulled up to the house in their jam-packed station wagon. Because the house had sat so long, the yard was overgrown, and the house looked dirty—especially the windows. The wind, rain, and hot sun had done a number on what was once clear glass.

When she got inside, Brenda was even more bothered by those dusty, stained, and spotted windows. She couldn't see clearly through them. The view was cloudy, almost like it was out of focus. Brenda decided the first thing she had to do was clean the windows!

Did you know sin makes our hearts look just like those dirty windows? Sin spots and stains our hearts, often making us want to turn from God because we sense we are unclean. Sin also clouds our outlook on life. It makes us focus on our shortcomings and our failures, making us feel like we can't live up to God's expectations.

Yet, sin can also make us more intensely aware of our need for God and the loving forgiveness he offers to us. When we confess our sins to the Lord, the Bible says he will forgive us. He will wash us white as snow, and he'll even forget what we did! God will wash the dirty windows of our hearts and make us clean once again! The best way to keep your heart's window spick-and-span is to wash it every day. Every night before you go to sleep, mentally run through the day's activities. Did you disobey your folks, tell a little white lie to your teacher, purposely forget to return your friend's tape because you didn't want to buy it yourself? Are there, in fact, things you did wrong you need to tell the Lord about and ask his forgiveness for? Do it right then. Wake up each morning with the "Son" shining brightly in your heart.

Dear Lord, sometimes my sins seem so great that I feel separated from you. My vision gets cloudy. I don't understand how you can love me. Yet, when I fall at your feet asking forgiveness of all my wrongs, you promise to cleanse me. Thank you, Lord, for washing me white as new fallen snow. Amen.

Prime Time This Week

Scripture tells us that everyone has sinned and fallen short of God's glory. Because of our sinful state, God had to send Jesus to die for us. He paid the penalty for our sin! When we accept Jesus as Lord and Savior, through him our sins are forgiven. Becoming a Christian doesn't mean you'll never sin again. You will, but your aim is to be obedient! That's why we have Jesus. This week let's see what else you can learn about sin and how to stay away from it.

Monday

How does sin occur? James 1:14–15 says it starts with a temptation that leads to lust (uncontrolled desire), which then leads you to sin. Quench the fire while it's still a flicker! Get rid of your temptations, and you'll get rid of sin! Think back and write an example of how something you did wrong started with a temptation that you gave in to! _____

_____

_____

_____

Prime Prayer: Pray that you'll recognize temptation for what it is and that God will give you the strength to say no right then, before the flicker of temptation becomes the fire of sin.

Tuesday

Read Isaiah 59:2. Sin separates us from God. Sin is evil and God is holy. They are opposites! See Psalm 5:4. Confessed sin brings you back into fellowship with your heavenly Father. Do you keep stumbling over the same sin? What is it? Read Hebrews 12:1. What does it tell you to do? _____

_____

_____

_____

Prime Prayer: Pray to remember to confess your sins instantly so your relationship with God can be restored. Then get rid of whatever keeps tripping you up.

Wednesday

The psalmist was not afraid to come before the Lord and ask God to reveal his sin to him and then to cleanse his heart. Read Psalm 51:10 and Psalm 139:23–24. Remember God is *for* you! _____

_____

_____

_____

Prime Prayer: Ask God to show you areas in your life that aren't pleasing to him. Allow him to cleanse your heart as you confess and turn away from your sin.

Thursday

Why do you feel so rotten when you know you've done wrong? You've been convicted! But, by whom? Read Proverbs 20:27 and John 16:8–9. How does the Holy Spirit help you stay on track? _____

_____

_____

_____

Prime Prayer: Ask the Holy Spirit to keep doing his job so you'll stay on the right track!

Friday

Read Romans 6:5–8:17. What does it teach you about sin? Now check out Galatians 5:16–25. What is the benefit of walking by the Spirit of God? _____

_____

_____

_____

Prime Prayer: Ask the Lord to give you power over sin as you *choose* to walk by the Spirit and not fulfill the desires of your fleshly, sinful nature.

This week's memory verse: Pick it! Write it! Remember it!

_____

_____

_____

_____

Lifestyles of the Rich and Famous

> For the love of money is the first step toward all kinds of sin. Some people have even turned away from God because of their love for it, and as a result have pierced themselves with many sorrows.
>
> 1 Timothy 6:10 TLB

All right, I confess. Many times while flipping through the television channels, I've gotten stuck on the exquisitely gorgeous homes and habits shown off by Robin Leach on "Lifestyles of the Rich and Famous." Though the tastes of the stars range from antique lamps to crystal chandeliers, mansions with imported-tile pools to dusty horse ranches, you'll always see a captivating display of unique possessions. A single half-hour show can leave the average person feeling like a poor old unknown nobody who lives in a hut, swims in a puddle, and drives a motorized heap of metal with wheels.

Yet, as I think back, I don't ever recall hearing any of those big stars with big bucks give credit or honor to

God for the talents that earned them the money to buy the things they own.

It is very common for people who start earning lots of money to make money more important in their lives than God. They don't have time or room in their lives for Jesus. They love money, not God who owns all the world and its possessions.

Loving money not only turns people away from God, but it also makes them competitive, selfish, and prideful. All of these can lead to sin, causing further separation from God.

The rich and famous, however, will often be the first to admit that after years of chasing careers and money, they're unhappy. You see, having the biggest house, the fastest car, or the fanciest clothes does not satisfy a person's inner hunger. Only a personal relationship with God's Son, Jesus, can do that. When I was modeling for the Wilhelmina Modeling Agency in New York, I met many rich and famous people. One actor in particular comes to my mind. He had wealth and worldwide fame, but he was still searching for the real meaning in life. I still pray for him, hoping he will turn his heart toward God.

Being rich and famous isn't all it's cracked up to be. Psalm 37:16 suggests it's much better to have a little money and be a Christian, than to own much and be ungodly. I agree.

Dear Lord, I can see that it's far better to keep you as number one in my life. Keep me from idolizing what others own and grateful for what you've graciously given me. Amen.

Prime Time This Week

Thousands of people have sacrificed precious and often irreplaceable things to get the best job, invest in the hottest deal, whatever it takes to get the almighty dollar. Families have suffered because of a workaholic parent or one who travels a lot to earn bonuses. Many families have split up because of arguments about money.

Worse yet, people, especially teens, who lack money, have gone so far as to steal to get it. Money becomes a god to many people. Loving money ruins people. The Bible offers wise advice about money matters. Take heed.

Monday

Many people are like the man Jesus talks about in Luke 12:15–21. Their life is spent building bigger houses, buying fancier cars, and so on. What warning does Jesus give these people? What does it mean to be rich toward God? Also read 1 Timothy 6:17–19. _____

_____

_____

_____

Prime Prayer: Pray today for wealthy people who are focused on themselves that they will have a changed heart, be willing to share, be generous, and use their money for others.

Tuesday

Do you have some favorite things that you treasure? Or maybe some special times that you hold dear in your heart? Read Luke 12:34 and Matthew 6:19–21. What kinds of things could be treasures that can be kept in heaven? _____

_____

_____

_____

Prime Prayer: Ask the Lord to help you store up treasures in heaven like your salvation, leading someone to Christ, helping others, and loving your family.

Wednesday

Most people believe that if they are generous and give away money, they'll run out! God says that's not true! Read Proverbs 11:25 and 2 Corinthians 9:6–11. Remember: To sow means to give! What is the best attitude to have about giving? _____

_____

_____

_____

Prime Prayer: Ask Jesus to teach you to give so he can bless you even more, plus to help you have a cheerful attitude about sharing.

Thursday

Read Hebrews 13:5. Are you content with what you have? Do you want more and better items? Do you constantly ask your parents for money or new clothes? Do you need to work on your attitude of gratitude? Does this verse imply that having Jesus is better than all else?

_____

_____

_____

_____

Prime Prayer: Ask God to help you see that in him you have everything because he makes you happy on the inside. Pray to be content and thankful for what you have.

Friday

Here's a toughy for most people. God asks you to tithe the money you earn, whether it's from a job or baby-sitting or your allowance! To tithe means to give God 10 percent of the total amount. So, if you earn $10, God gets $1. Get it? Now read Proverbs 3:9–10 and Malachi 3:10. How does God promise to reward you for obedient tithing? _____

_____

_____

Prime Prayer: Ask the Lord to help you understand that a portion of the money you earn goes to him as a way of furthering the work of the church and also as a way to thank him for helping you earn it in the first place!

This week's memory verse: Pick it! Write it! Remember it!

_____

_____

_____

_____

Spiritual Development

Serving Up
a Spiritual Meal

My nourishment comes from doing the will of
God who sent me, and from finishing his work.

John 4:34 TLB

What's your favorite meal? Spicy spaghetti, Mexican enchiladas, barbecued chicken, charbroiled hamburgers, piping hot pizza? And your after-dinner treat? Which desserts top your list? A hot fudge brownie sundae, strawberry shortcake, creamy cheesecake, apple pie? It's so simple for us to think of all the delicious foods we can feed ourselves physically. But what about spiritually?

Jesus told his disciples in this week's Scripture that he had a different kind of food. He explained to his followers that his nourishment came from serving God, doing what was pleasing to his Father. Well, certainly he wasn't referring to physical food to eat. He was talking about spiritual nourishment, spiritual food for our spiritual selves.

Yes, our spiritual selves need nutrition, too. Each of us has a spiritual nature that hungers for God. Some describe it as a God-shaped void that only God himself can fill.

Many people get wrapped up in the wrong things in their attempts to nourish the spiritual hunger inside of them: cults, wrong spirits, alcohol, drugs, overindulging in TV, movies, or music. They know they need something, but they can't figure out or admit what their need really is. It is God!

Let's look at a menu for nourishing your spiritual self. The first course you should serve is Jesus. Simply ask him to come and live in your heart. When you do this, you are forgiven and you become one with God and have peace with him. You are new inside, or born again. Your spirit is what becomes new. Jesus says in John 6:35 that he is the bread of life and that if we have him, we will not be spiritually hungry. Just as we don't eat food once and then never again, so we must not fill up once on Jesus and then call it enough. We need to feed on him daily!

The second course is the Holy Spirit. In this way you can experience the fruit or the characteristics of the Holy Spirit in your life: love, joy, peace, patience, kindness, goodness, faithfulness, gentleness, and self-control. We have these great qualities in us because Jesus lives in us.

As a third course, serve your spirit the Word of God. This is straight spiritual food that your spirit needs. The Bible is your handbook to life. It teaches you and guides you according to God's will for your life. Jesus said his food was to do the will of his Father God (John 4:34).

The same applies to us. It feeds our spirit to learn and to do God's will.

And now for your spiritual dessert! Fellowship. Spending time with other Christians. Finding out what God has done and is doing in the lives of others helps your faith to grow and nourishes your spirit.

Jesus, the Holy Spirit, the Word of God, Christian fellowship—a well-balanced spiritual meal!

> Father, it's so easy for me to forget about feeding my spiritual self, but I know it needs nourishment to be able to help me grow and be a stronger Christian. Help me. Amen.

Prime Time This Week

The world screams for your attention. Your life is busy and full. Yet, you must make God top priority. It's more than just needing to make room for God in your life. It's making *him* your life. God won't come barging in on you. You will need to invite him. Your spirit needs to commune with God's Spirit in order to grow. They need to be together. It won't happen in front of the TV or strolling the mall. It takes a decision. You are the key.

Monday

Do you know people who try to fill their inner God-shaped void with other things? What do they try? Read Galatians 5:19–21; Colossians 3:5–10; and Ephesians 4:14. Do these sound familiar? They never worked back then, and they still won't satisfy people today! _____

_____

_____

Prime Prayer: Ask God to keep you from filling yourself with worthless things and to feed only on him.

Tuesday

Jesus said he had a different kind of food. There was something he did that fed his spirit. Read John 4:34 to discover Jesus' secret snack! Describe what he did. ___

_____

_____

_____

Prime Prayer: Ask God to show you his will so you can do it like Jesus did, and feel the satisfaction from obedience.

Wednesday

What can happen to a person who stops feeding on or communing with the Lord? Find out in 1 Kings 11:1–10. What was Solomon's downfall? How can you avoid his mistake? _____

_____

_____

_____

Prime Prayer: Pray to be obedient to God's instruction so you'll stay close to Jesus.

Thursday

A spiritual meal has four food groups just like a well-balanced dinner. Jesus, the Holy Spirit, the Bible, and Christian fellowship. Which of the four do you need an extra helping of? Jesus wants you to get a well-balanced meal each day! _____

_____

_____

_____

_____

Prime Prayer: Ask the Lord to help you remember to get a well-balanced spiritual meal each day.

Friday

Receiving communion at church is often referred to as a "spiritual meal." What is the spiritual meaning for sharing in communion? Find out in 1 Corinthians 11:23–26. How is communion important to you? ____

_____

_____

_____

_____

Prime Prayer: Pray that each time you receive communion you'll remember what Jesus has done on the cross for you. He is truly worthy of your praise.

This week's memory verse: Pick it! Write it! Remember it!

_____

_____

_____

_____

Lighten Up Your Heart

Anxiety in the heart of a man weighs it down, but a good word makes it glad.

Proverbs 12:25 NASB

Cindy felt sad. School wasn't going the way it used to. She had always been a pretty good student, but this last semester was tough for her. It wasn't just that her cocky psychology teacher, Mr. Marcus, was making life impossible for her because she didn't see eye-to-eye with his viewpoints. It was also chemistry class. Cindy couldn't make up her mind which combustive chemical she should report on, making her last-minute paper a flop. She was falling so far behind. Cindy's heart was heavy. She felt so down about school. For the first time she wondered if she was going to crash and burn this semester, sending her GPA on a downward spiral.

But, it wasn't just school. Her friendship with Melissa was getting to her. No matter what she did, she was always wrong and Melissa was always right! After a while, Cindy just wasn't herself. She moped around, spending most of her time in her bedroom with her earphones on. She didn't care about Melissa and her other friends like she used to. Staying home was fine with her. Frankly speaking, Cindy was depressed!

Have you recently felt like Cindy? Are you down in the dumps? Got the blues? Are you struggling with depression and discouragement? Are you not acting like yourself? Feel like pulling away from everyone or going out and getting blasted to escape? You may be depressed! Proverbs 12:25 tells us that anxiety, worry, and depression make our heart feel like someone tied it to a big boulder and threw it in the lake! Depression is a common emotion among teenage girls, but it doesn't have to stick around. There are ways to chase it out of your life!

How can your heavy heart lighten up? Scripture tells us that a good word of encouragement will do the trick. No one needs another put-down. They need a word to put them up! Where can we go to get a good, uplifting word that will take the weight off a heavy heart? Check these out.

First, the Bible can be your best friend when it comes to good, positive words. And it's always right there for you! Open it up and start reading.

Second, your pastor, priest, or youth director is also familiar with the Bible and can share some Scriptures with you that will lift you up. Pastors have a gentle, listening ear. If they didn't care, they wouldn't be in that profession!

Third, to many school teachers and counselors, teaching is more than just a job. They love teens! Test the waters. Open up a little bit and see if they respond with encouraging words and trust.

Fourth, parents and close friends know your moods and are sensitive to your feelings. They may have just the perfect word to cheer you up. If you're hanging out with downbeat kids, better think about switching friends.

Fifth, is YOU! What you say to yourself in the silence of your mind will affect how you feel. Thoughts like, *I'm so dumb, I'm a nothing,* and *Life stinks!* won't make you feel better. Try, *I may have messed up, but next time I'll do better,* or *I'm a good person; I know myself better than they do, things will get better with God's help.* Your self-talk has about a 99.9 percent effect on how you feel about yourself, your circumstances, and others in your life. Control your thoughts. Don't let them control you! Encouraging words will start the crane cranking to lift that heavy boulder off your heart and drop it on the head of depression itself!

Dear Lord, sometimes life gets me down. It seems like everything goes wrong. I know you want me to be happy, so when I turn to you and others who care, send encouraging words my way. And help me to be an encouragement to others. Amen.

Prime Time This Week

Depression doesn't have the right to control your life or that of a friend or family member. Overcoming depression does take effort and action. You must *choose* to attack feelings of depression. Force it out! You may have a hard time getting started—you will have to do what you don't *feel* like doing *before* you feel like doing it. So here we go. Lights, camera, ACTION!

Monday

First, always go to the Lord with your feelings and problems. He cares more than anyone! What does Psalm 34:18–19 and Psalm 27:5 promise to God's people who are down in the dumps? _____

_____

_____

_____

Prime Prayer: Ask God to remind you at the times you feel depressed that he is with you and will lift you up.

Tuesday

Life not going your way? Are your expectations unrealistic? Be flexible! Read Proverbs 16:9 and Isaiah 55:8–9. You might make plans, but who determines the final outcome? Accept the Lord's plans. Only he can see the big picture! _____

_____

_____

_____

Prime Prayer: Ask God to help you to be open to his plans for your day, your week, and your life, knowing he can be trusted with your life.

Wednesday

Do you have *anahedia?* Huh? *Anahedia* is a lack of joy in your life! Most depressed people don't feel too joyful. Where can you get joy? Read Psalm 16:11. Right now you are in God's presence! Draw your joy from him.

_____

_____

_____

_____

Prime Prayer: Pray that you will make more time to spend in God's presence—praying and praising him—so you will know real joy.

Thursday

A surefire way to get over being down is to get up and out! Increase your activities. Do stuff! Don't be alone. Seek out positive people and fun activities. Also, working out does wonders. Exercise releases depression-fighting hormones. Fifteen minutes a day will start brightening your outlook. Make a list of some activities you would like to get involved in. Also make a workout schedule for the week. Try a different form of exercise each day so you don't get bored (walking, jumping rope, skating, biking, jogging, aerobic dancing, and so on). _____

_____

_____

_____

Prime Prayer: Ask God to help you get up and work out when you feel blue. Thank him for making your body able to fight depression.

Friday

Are you still sitting in life's low seat? Don't be too proud or too afraid to seek professional help. We all have times in our lives when a trained counselor is necessary. Don't give up! Talk it over with your parents.

_____

_____

_____

Prime Prayer: Ask God to put someone in your life who will understand what you are going through and who will help you work it out.

This week's memory verse: Pick it! Write it! Remember it!

_____

_____

_____

_____

_____

Let's Get Busy

God has given each of you some special abilities;
be sure to use them to help each other, passing on
to others God's many kinds of blessings.

1 Peter 4:10 TLB

Kelly was introduced to gymnastics when her mom enrolled her in "Tumblin' Toddlers Class" for four-year-olds at the local community center. It was love at first somersault! Kelly started private training in grade school. Her coordination, skill, and graceful control were evident. Kelly earned high scores at local, regional, and state gymnastic meets. She was a natural. Her coaches were well aware of her abilities and were preparing her step by step for the U.S. Olympic team.

But when Kelly was in junior high a snag in the plans came up. She had spent many years and thousands of hours polishing routines and perfecting moves. Those were precious hours, but they could have been spent with her friends. Kelly missed out on football games, class dances, church camp, and sleep-overs, all because she had to keep fine-tuned for her competitive sport. But when Kelly couldn't go on the eighth-grade graduation trip because of a state meet, she had had it. She wanted to be free to hang out with her friends at the mall or movies without worrying about getting home early on Friday nights for Saturday's workout or competition. The pressure Kelly was getting from her parents and coaches not to quit made her more determined to do whatever she wanted.

What Kelly interpreted as "pressure" was really justified concern. The coaches didn't want Kelly to quit gymnastics and waste her God-given talent just to "hang out" with her friends.

I've known many girls like Kelly. Marcie excelled on the keyboard, Lindsey in drawing, and Maggie in ballet. Each of them shelved their talent for the sake of their social life. They just wanted to hang loose! To be idle.

Kelly and the others may have felt their practice life was cheating them out of some fun times. But, in the long run, who gets cheated?

For one, God does. If a person has exceptional natural abilities, it is a blessed gift from God. He wants them to develop and use the talent for him. Being idle is not God's plan for his children. Perhaps God's plan for Kelly was to be a witness for him on the women's U.S. Olympic team. Maybe a special spot was prepared for Marcia to play in a Christian band. If we ignore our talents, are we being unfair to God?

Second, the girls don't know the real feeling of being cheated until they realize they temporarily followed the wrong path for their life. Thoughts of what they could have accomplished have plagued people for centuries. They wasted their time and their lives producing nothing.

What about you? Do you have a talent that you're ignoring? Does the self-discipline seem too tough? Are you wasting time, coasting through life? Will you be one of the millions who look back with nothing but wasted days and wasted nights to show for their teen years because all they wanted to do was "hang out"? Give it some thought. Discover, uncover, or recover that gift God has planted in you!

Oh, Lord, have I been overlooking the gifts and talents you have placed in me because it's easier to coast and not care? I desire to get on the right road and use what you have given me to bring praise and honor to your name. Amen.

Prime Time This Week

The Drifters and The Coasters were popular singing groups in the sixties. Their names reflected the attitude of their generation. They just wouldn't fit today. The people of the nineties are active! At least, most of them are. Hangin' out, sitting around with too much time on your hands is okay for a while. But when kids aren't pursuing their interests and talents, extra time becomes idle. Idle time has driven tons of teens straight to juvenile hall. They come up with stuff to do to fill their time, but the wrong kind of stuff! If you find yourself preferring to hang around, jump in and join the nineties generation. Make Arsenio Hall's slogan yours and "Let's get busy!"

Monday

The Bible's description of an excellent woman has something to say about idleness. See Proverbs 31:27. Is she idle? No way. She is energetic and always occupied with a worthwhile project. You can be productive and still have fun! Sew, bake, garden, bike, teach a kid how to swim, or play tennis or softball. Name some projects that you'd like to take up or already do. _____

_____

_____

_____

Prime Prayer: Ask Jesus to give you ideas to keep you busy, producing things and good qualities in you.

Tuesday

Idle time gives you time to gossip. God says "no good" to that one! First Timothy 5:13 calls some women busybodies. A busybody is so *un*-busy, she has her nose in *everybody else's* business! Watch what happens when your friends get together and veg out. Be careful what you say about others. Why do you think God is against gossip? _____

_____

_____

_____

Prime Prayer: Pray for the ability to stop gossip instead of spreading it. Ask God to give you creative ideas that will keep you and your friends occupied.

Wednesday

If you don't work, you don't eat! That's life in the real world. Just wait until you're out on your own. What does Proverbs 19:15 say about how an idle person will suffer? Now read the parable in Matthew 20:6. What answer would you give God if he asked you the same question? _____

_____

_____

_____

Prime Prayer: Ask God to make you a hard worker, not a handout taker. Working hard impresses parents, bosses, friends, and the Lord. Go for it.

Thursday

Beware of the two terrible time stealers: television and telephone. (It's a tongue twister if you say it fast!) Nothing wrong with relaxing once in a while to the tune of "The Wonder Years" or "Full House," but please, don't waste your brain on soaps or Geraldo and Oprah! Get smart. Tune into "20/20" and other great news or educational shows. List three programs you'll watch on television this week that are informational. Now the telephone. A tough one for girls! Set a timer. Don't tie up the lines all night! _____

_____

_____

_____

Prime Prayer: Ask the Lord to make you aware of how you spend your time. Aim to value the precious time he has given you. Make the most of it.

Friday

"Think I'll take a little nap." Think twice, my friend! Tons of teens sleep their way through life. Get a hobby. Get a job. Get a life! Read Proverbs 6:9–10. Too much sleep is a sign of laziness, depression, or mono! Do you sleep after school and get up at noon on Saturdays? If you're sick—see a doc! If you're in the dumps—talk it out! If you're lazy—watch out! _____

_____

_____

_____

Prime Prayer: Ask the Lord to teach you to be diligent, not lazy. He will reward you!

This week's memory verse: Pick it! Write it! Remember it!

_____

_____

_____

_____

_____

Angels

"You're Such an Angel"

For he orders his angels to protect you wherever
you go.

Psalm 91:11 TLB

Little girls have heard this phrase for centuries. When
they clean up their room, dry the dishes, put away their
Barbies, walk the dog, perform well in school, watch
over baby brother, Mom and Dad reward them with
these four little words: "You're such an angel!" and then
a hug and a kiss. Yes, girls are called angels when they
are helpful without complaining about it, or when they
surprise their parents by doing something delightfully
good without being asked.

As we grow up, we think of angels in the same way.
Surely they are just sweet, kind, always cheerful do-
gooders who float on cotton-candy clouds all day. What
concept do you have of angels? Do you doubt their exis-
tence, or do you think they are only in heaven, completely unavailable to us, God's children?

I have found most teens have a lot of unanswered
questions about God's heavenly host of angels. For

instance, does every person really have a guardian angel? What is the purpose of angels? Are they always invisible? Do they talk? Do they have names? Do they fight wars? What do they look like? Are they ranked in any special order? Do they worship God because they have to, or want to? Do they really have wings? On and on. Have you ever asked any of these questions? If so, congratulations! Inquisitive minds want to know. And they'll find out!

If you've been the kind to just blow off the idea of angels, thinking they are make-believe, then get ready. You're about to learn some exciting stuff! For instance, one of the main jobs of God's angels is to watch over and protect you! Angels are available to guard you, to keep you from harm. All you have to do is ask God to send the angels to surround you. You also need to be realistic. If you decide to do something ridiculous like diving off the Empire State Building, don't expect a big burly angel to catch you halfway down and softly deliver you to the sidewalk below. Angels protect God's people when they are doing his work and are obedient to his Word.

This week you will be discovering valuable information about angels that will change your view of these majestic creatures.

> Dear Lord, open my eyes concerning the truth about angels. Convince me of their reality, so I will confidently call on their assistance. Amen.

Prime Time This Week

Angel! The word itself means "messenger of God." That's right! Angels are God's personal messengers. They await God's instruction, then fly (yes, they have wings

[Ezekiel 10:5]) off to their destination and deliver a message or intervene in a situation to protect God's plan from being stopped. Angels are alive and well. Sound unbelievable? Remember who they are working for! With God, all things are possible! Now, let's answer all those questions.

Monday

What is the main purpose of angels? To bring messages from God to believers and to minister to God's children. Read Hebrews 1:14; Genesis 28:12; and Revelation 1:1. What was the angel's message to Mary Magdalene in Matthew 28:1–7? Take note: Angels *do* talk and they do appear to people! Check out Hebrews 13:2!

_____

_____

_____

_____

Prime Prayer: Pray that you will be more aware of angelic activity, remembering that a kind stranger may be an angel!

Tuesday

Are angels also assigned by God to guard and protect people? What is the answer according to Psalm 34:7 and Exodus 23:20? Now read the story of Daniel's night at "Lions' Den Inn" in Daniel 6:16–23. What purpose did the angel serve? _____

_____

_____

Prime Prayer: Ask the Lord to help you remember that his angels are there waiting for you to call on them for protection. Each day ask God to send his angels to watch over you.

Wednesday

Do angels fight wars? Yes! They fight against the evil forces of Satan! Read Revelation 12:7–9. Some angels are even known as destroying angels. Read about them in 1 Chronicles 21:15–16 and Psalm 78:49. How does it make you feel knowing God's angels are on your side?

_____

_____

_____

_____

Prime Prayer: Ask God today to send his angels to fight the evil one on your behalf. Now thank him that powerful angels are on your side!

Thursday

Where do angels live? Read Mark 13:32. Do they have names? Find out in Luke 1:26 and Luke 2:21. Do they freely worship the Lord? See Luke 2:13–14. _____

_____

_____

_____

Prime Prayer: Ask God to help you be like the angels by praising him every day and every night.

Friday

Are angels ranked in any special order? Find out about the angel Michael in Daniel 10:13 and Jude 9 (*arch* means "chief"). Do you know any hymns that refer to cherubim and seraphim? Cherubim are angels of the second highest rank, while seraphim are the highest order of angels. What do Ezekiel 10:16 and Isaiah 6:2 have to say? _____

_____

_____

_____

Prime Prayer: Spend a few moments thanking God for the new understanding you have of angels and what they mean in the life of a Christian.

This week's memory verse: Pick it! Write it! Remember it!

_____

_____

_____

_____

_____

Dealing with Death

Death . . .
The Beginning of Life

> I say emphatically that anyone who listens to my message and believes in God who sent me has eternal life, and will never be damned for his sins, but has already passed out of death into life.
>
> John 5:24 TLB

Mindy had been a brave soldier watching her friend Amanda die from cancer. They had practically grown up together. They loved the same clothes, listened to the same music, and usually both liked the same guy! Together they watched many movies, ate pizzas, and jammed phone lines for hours! But now all of that seemed far away. Mindy stood looking at the body, the shell, of her best friend who had gone to be with Jesus. She felt content knowing Amanda wasn't there. In fact, the made-up body didn't even look like her. The real Amanda was gone. She was with her heavenly Father.

As Mindy stepped away from the casket, she took her place near the microphone, waiting her turn. She sweetly sang a song in honor of her friendship with Amanda. The song talked about friends being friends forever when Jesus is their Lord.

See, Mindy knew her dear friend loved the Lord Jesus and that she was now in heaven. She also knew that when she died, she would be with Amanda again. Surprisingly, Mindy found herself secretly excited for Amanda because she was starting a new life. Eternal life. A life in heaven that would never end. Amanda's spirit was alive and well, just not present on earth anymore.

Death is a hard experience to deal with. Many teens have seen their grandparents, parents, or a friend pass away. At times you probably have your own fears and unanswered questions about death. The Bible gives believers reassuring insights on death that will help you understand it better. Death may appear to be so final. In reality, it is just the beginning of a brand-new life.

Dear Lord, because I listen to you and believe in you, I know I will spend eternity in heaven with you when my life here is over. Teach me your views on death, so I will better understand it. Amen.

Prime Time This Week

Funeral services for Christians have changed in recent years. As people better understand God's view of death, they come to realize that death is not the end but a beginning. The beginning of life in the very presence of God. That is cause for praise and rejoicing. Sure, mourning death is normal, but for a Christian, a funeral is a celebration. Today you'll find more singing, more laughter, and brighter colors gracing the funeral parlor or church. The loved one is gone, but knowing where they have gone and whom they will be with, helps ease the pain of missing them. Let's see what the Bible says.

Monday

Exactly how does God view the death of his children? To find out, read Psalm 116:15. Why do you think God feels this way? How does knowing this help you deal with death? _____

_____

_____

_____

Prime Prayer: Ask God to help you view death as he does.

Tuesday

Physical death is not the end of the road for Christians. They have spiritual life, eternal life in heaven! What does John 14:2 tell you? _____

_____

_____

_____

Prime Prayer: Thank God today for preparing a special place in heaven for each of us!

Wednesday

Christians are never alone in the death process. Read Psalm 23:4. We can rest assured that God is with us in all we go through. How does this fact comfort you? _____

_____

_____

_____

Prime Prayer: Ask God to remind you that in each person's "valley of death," he is holding their hand every step of the way.

Thursday

When a person dies, those left behind grieve. What does Matthew 5:4 promise to those who are in mourning over the loss of a loved one? Also read 2 Corinthians 1:3–5. Are you suffering a loss? Who can comfort you? _____

_____

_____

_____

Prime Prayer: Ask God to comfort those who are mourning today.

Friday

Live your earthly life to the fullest! Have zeal! Zeal is an eager interest in the pursuit of life. Does Jesus want you to have a dull, empty life? See John 10:10 and 1 Corinthians 10:31. _____

_____

_____

_____

Prime Prayer: Ask Jesus to give you enthusiasm and passion for life, to live it to the fullest, taking advantage of the opportunities he gives you.

This week's memory verse: Pick it! Write it! Remember it!

_____

_____

_____

_____

_____

Trick-or-Treat

And no wonder, for even Satan disguises himself
as an angel of light. Therefore it is not surprising
if his servants also disguise themselves as servants
of righteousness; whose end shall be according to
their deeds.

2 Corinthians 11:14–15 NASB

My husband recently had the privilege of delivering
the junior sermon for the children in our church. He
held up a brown paper sack, and then slowly pulled out
a plate of freshly made, hot, ready-to-eat donut holes.
The kids oohed and aahed. A sugary sweet donut hole—
the perfect Sunday morning snack and a great reward
for coming to church. *That Pastor Bill,* they thought,
what a nice guy to bring us donut holes.

Before giving each child a donut, Bill asked for a vol-
unteer to test them. Hands went shooting into the air.
A lucky young boy was selected. As his teeth sunk deep
into the donut, his tongue got a good taste of what
appeared to be sugar. YUCK! It was salt!

The salty donut hole looked exactly like the sweet
sugary ones. The treat turned out to be a trick.

Second Corinthians 11:14–15 tells of a similar situation where what looks like a treat is really a trick. Satan and his servants make themselves out to look like God's angels and servants. They wear a disguise, hoping you can't tell the difference. Through the years, subtle, deceptive, so-called churches and organizations fool people into believing they are Christian groups when really their underlying motive is to lead people away from Christ. The same can be true of situations. It looks safe enough on the surface, but underneath there's trouble.

For instance, you may think rock concerts, beer parties, "illegal" help on a test, a secret date with a guy your parents dislike are all tasty little treats. But watch out! It may backfire in your face and turn out to be an ugly trick of the enemy.

God does not trick his children. He does not need to wear a disguise trying to make himself look like someone he's not. He is trustworthy. Your heavenly Father wants you to know him, so you won't ever confuse a treat of his with a trick of Satan.

Oh Father, help me to keep my eyes open and my heart focused on you so that I won't be led astray by Satan's tricky tactics. Amen.

Prime Time This Week

An army will never win the war if it doesn't know who the enemy is or how he works. What are his tactics? His favorite moves? As a member of the army of God, you must be able to recognize your enemy: Satan. He's not a funny-looking guy in a red suit with horns with a pointed tail and holding a pitchfork! He is real, alive, and roaming around planet earth! Be wise to him. Take your blinders off and see him for who he really is. He works through others, trying to lead people away from Christ. Study up. God doesn't want you to be ignorant!

Monday

Exactly what is Satan's goal here on earth? Read John 10:10. Satan wants to destroy the kingdom of God and the lives of Christians. Why? He is absolutely 100 percent evil! Read Psalm 97:10 and Psalm 34:13–14. How does God feel about evil and our participation in it? _____

_____

_____

_____

Prime Prayer: Ask God to help you recognize evil and to stay far away from it by drawing closer to him.

Tuesday

Satan has always been in a power struggle with God. Read the description of Satan's selfish desire to be better than God. Notice each sentence begins with "I will . . ." Find this in Isaiah 14:13–14. What is it that Satan wants? Remember, God always wins! His Spirit is in us and gives us authority over Satan. See 1 John 4:4. Who is in us and who is in the world? _____

_____

_____

_____

Prime Prayer: Ask God to help you to change your "I will" to "Thy will" and submit yourself to God's authority.

Wednesday

Read 2 Peter 2:1–3. In today's world many musicians have become false teachers, leading teens away from the teachings of Christ. Yet, most teens ignorantly defend their favorite singers. But you can't believe everything you hear! Well, here's how to test their words and their life-styles. Read 1 John 4:1–3. If the musicians you listen to do not honor God and do not say Jesus is Lord, they are not on God's team. Watch Al Menconi's videotape called *Everything You Always Wanted to Know about Rock Music.* Don't be fooled. What musicians do you currently listen to? What are the main themes of their songs? Do they honor God? Which group do you think God wants you to quit listening to? _____

_____

_____

_____

Prime Prayer: Ask the Lord to open your eyes to false teaching and eliminate it from your life.

Thursday

Read 1 Thessalonians 2:18. Does Satan try to stop God's plan in *your* life as he did in Paul's? Absolutely! Use your authority over him when he gets in your way, tries to tempt you, or puts evil thoughts in your head. Tell him to leave in the name of Jesus! Read Matthew 4:10. What did Satan do when Jesus told him to get lost?

Check out Matthew 6:13. Can Christians ask God to protect them from Satan and his evil plans? _____

_____

_____

_____

Prime Prayer: Ask God to protect you from evil and the evil one! Tell Satan to get lost—you are God's property!

Friday

According to God's Word, the world is black and white. People are either for God or against him, good or evil. Read Luke 11:23. Who do you know who opposes God? _____

_____

_____

_____

Prime Prayer: Ask God to open the hearts of your family and friends who need to know him personally.

This week's memory verse: Pick it! Write it! Remember it!

_____

_____

_____

_____

_____

Praising the Lord!

Praise . . . Just Do It!

Let everything alive give praises to the Lord! You praise him! Hallelujah!

Psalm 150:6 TLB

When you were a little kid, did you ever attend vacation Bible school at your church? Can you remember singing "Jesus Loves Me" or "Praise Him" or "Father, I Adore You"? Little kids are so free to sing and clap and praise the Lord. Their hearts are pure, their motives are right.

Then they grow up. They become teenagers. Too cool to show they love God, too afraid of what others might think of them. Trying to get a group of thirteen- to six-teen-year-olds to sing love songs to Jesus is like trying to land a seaplane in the sand. No way! But why? Are others really more valuable than the Lord?

Every year millions of teens attend rock concerts and wave their hands in the air to their music stars. In a sense, they are praising them. Even Christian teens find themselves idolizing these artists who really are anti-Christ in their beliefs. Yet, they can't seem to get into

95

praising the very One who loves them, saves them, and is the key to their often troubled lives. Well, what about praising the "true rock," Jesus Christ?

Psalm 150:6 says that everything that is alive or is breathing gives praise to the Lord. Pinch yourself! Are you alive? Great! You qualify. God wants *you* to praise him!

Why should you praise the Lord? Glad you asked! Praising the Lord helps you focus on him. That allows your problems and troubles to drift away, putting your trials in perspective. Praising God gives you new strength, courage, and hope. Praise also makes you feel closer to God and more aware of his presence in your life. In fact, the Bible tells us that God inhabits, or lives in, the praises of his people. When you praise God, he is right there with you! Praising the Lord benefits you, his child, but it also makes his heart glad. Take some quiet time alone. Praise God for all the blessings he has given you. Praise him for what he has done. Praise him because he is Lord. Praise him. Just do it!

Dear Lord, you alone are worthy of my praise and adoration. Help me to feel less self-conscious about praising you, thanking you, and loving you. You mean so much to me. Amen.

Prime Time This Week

Let's get practical. Exactly *how* do you praise the Lord? The Bible says to make a joyful noise to him. Lots of definitions could fit *joyful noise*. Your voice doesn't have to be perfectly on key or tuned up with the guy next to you. The Bible just says to sing—croak, if you want—just make it happy! And loud! Now add a few instruments if you want. Psalm 150 lists all kinds: guitar, trombones, cymbals, drums, organ, flute, and so on! You can stand, sit, kneel, raise your hands, or clap them! Want to do it alone? No problem. Buy a praise tape and cut loose!

Monday

God works in our lives daily. It's proper to praise him for things he does. Jesus and King David did! Read Matthew 11:25. What did Jesus praise God for? Now check out Psalm 40:1–3. David praised God for what? Now turn to John 17:4. Jesus said that he glorified God on earth by doing what? How can you glorify God today? _____

_____

_____

_____

Prime Prayer: Ask God to open your eyes to all things he does for you every day, to help you praise him for each of them, and to do his work.

Tuesday

Praise can actually release God's power to work in our lives. Praising God is the life source of our Christian faith. Read Acts 2:46–47. The Lord saved people and added to the number of Christians because the people did what? Do you need God to do something in your life? Pray and praise! Watch what happens. _____

_____

_____

_____

Prime Prayer: Tell the Lord the situation facing you, then praise him in order to allow his power to work through you.

Wednesday

Shout and dance praises to the Lord! You've got to be kidding! No, really! Praise can be quiet and reverent, but praise sessions in the Bible weren't like that! Read Psalm 66:1 and Psalm 98:4–6. How would you describe the noise level? Check out the movement level! Read Psalm 149:3 and Psalm 150:4. Be footloose for Jesus. Let his joy take over! If your church doesn't praise like this, ask why. Then have your own private praise party! _____

_____

_____

_____

Prime Prayer: Ask Jesus to show you how to get filled with his joy and to shout, sing, and dance your praises to him. Don't be shy!

Thursday

What does it mean to sacrifice something? Right. It means to give it up. Read Hebrews 13:15. How would you offer up a sacrifice of praise? It is a sacrifice because at first you may not *feel* like doing it, but you do it anyway, because it pleases God. How do you feel about praise? _____

_____

_____

_____

Prime Prayer: Ask the Lord to teach you to praise whether you feel like it or not, knowing it will lighten your heart and his.

Friday

Whistle a happy tune! Sing a praise to Jesus! James 5:13 says singing is the sign of a cheerful person. Actually it works both ways. You can sing praises because you *are* cheerful or to *get* cheerful. Remember, Satan hates praise! It's the perfect way to keep Satan off your back and out of your life. Practice praise today. How do you feel afterwards? _____

_____

_____

_____

Prime Prayer: Ask God to help you remember that praising him will cheer up your day.

This week's memory verse: Pick it! Write it! Remember it!

_____

_____

_____

_____

_____

Success

God's Formula for Success

> This book of the law shall not depart from your mouth, but you shall meditate on it day and night, so that you may be careful to do according to all that is written in it; for then you will make your way prosperous, and then you will have success.
>
> Joshua 1:8 NASB

Go to your local bookstore and you will find the shelves packed with books filled with advice on how to be successful! Of course, whether people are successful or not all depends on how they define the word *success*. Here is what a few teens had to say.

Patti told me, "I think I will feel successful if I am happy. It doesn't matter to me what I am doing or how much money I am making, but if I am smiling, I'm a success."

Jason felt this way: "My dad owns his own company. He is a very successful businessman and quite respected in our city. Following in his footsteps, I feel I had bet-

101

ter make something of myself or it will make my dad look like he didn't bring me up very well. I do want to make him proud of me."

Mike's viewpoint was, "Success is when all the bills are paid, you have a little extra money for the movies, but most important, you have success when your life is straight with God. If I screw up my life in every other area, it won't matter. My relationship to God is what matters most."

Patti, Jason, and Mike have different ways to measure their future success. The amount of success they each experience will depend on whether or not they live up to their own standards.

The world's view of success is to be in control, wealthy, educated, good-looking, and putting yourself first. God's view is different. He doesn't pressure us to be millionaires or professors. He challenges us to follow him. Following him, we will find success.

Joshua 1:8 (NASB) describes God's formula for success. The interesting fact about this verse is that when we obey the Lord and live at peace with him, he makes us prosperous by supplying all our needs and gives us a heart of love and joy. Our success can spread to every area of our life when we let the Lord in and follow his Word!

> Dear Jesus, my true desire is to keep my eyes on you and your Word, because in obedience to you I will have true success—both inside and outside. Amen.

Prime Time This Week

Once you're out of high school or college and in the work world, the pressure to succeed stares you in the face. At least you may feel that it does. Friends are watching. Employers are watching. Parents are watching. The thought of failing terrifies many teens as they look to their future. As a teen you can learn right now what God's formula for success is! Let's study the ingredients of the special recipe this week.

Monday

Joshua 1:8 says that prosperity comes from what? To meditate means to think deeply about something over and over. Reading, studying, memorizing. Hiding God's Word in your heart will light your path, direct you toward success. But just knowing God's Word is not enough. What does Psalm 119:105–6 (TLB) says you must do? _____

_____

_____

_____

Prime Prayer: Ask the Lord to give you the desire and the diligence to study and meditate on his Word, but most important, to obey it.

Tuesday

God told Joshua he would be successful if he meditated on the Word both day and night! In the morning and in the evening! Why is this such a key factor in God's plan for success? Why day and night? Read Proverbs 8:17 (KJV) and then Psalm 16:7. _____

_____

_____

_____

Prime Prayer: Ask God to help you make time in your schedule each morning and each evening to read his Word so that you may find him and hear from him even as you sleep.

Wednesday

Some people think you've become great and successful in life when you have others working under you or for you. Errand boys! Is it true? Are you to serve or be served? Find out in Matthew 20:26–28. Why do people who have "servant attitudes" usually have more friends? How do your friends and family respond when you do things for them? _____

_____

_____

_____

Prime Prayer: Ask God to give you a servant's heart and to help you start today to do things for others, putting them first and yourself second.

Thursday

According to Psalm 1:1–4, what are the key ingredients to prosperity? How does listening to evil and associating with the ungodly or a non-Christian, ruin a person's success? _____

_____

_____

_____

Prime Prayer: Ask God to make you aware of the ungodly counsel in your life so you can get rid of it and listen only to the wisdom of his people. Also, delight in God's laws so you, too, will be like a fruitful tree.

Friday

Success and prosperity are more than money and fame. Success in a Christian's life is about honoring God and living a life pleasing to him. It's also about inner success—having a heart filled with love, joy, peace, and contentment! How is inner success perhaps even more important to God than financial success? _____

_____

_____

_____

Prime Prayer: Ask God to help you live a life more pleasing to him so that your life will reflect inner success and you will be a true witness of God's love in your life.

This week's memory verse: Pick it! Write it! Remember it!

_____

_____

_____

_____

_____

Follow the Yellow Brick Road

> Where there is no vision, the people perish: but he
> that keepeth the law, happy is he.
>
> Proverbs 29:18 KJV

Remember the scarecrow in *The Wizard of Oz?* When
Dorothy first met him, he seemed rather confused.
When she asked him which way to the Land of Oz
where the great Wizard lived, he pointed in two different directions.

Do you ever feel like that straw-stuffed scarecrow?
Deciding which road to take in your life is a major decision. Today's world offers so many opportunities and
choices. Picking a path can get complicated. Yet, God's
Word tells us that without a vision, or direction, people
perish—or more simply put, they dry up and blow away!

One good way to get started on a direction is to set
goals. With goals, you will have a sense of purpose,
something to work toward. Choose goals that are realistic. If your goals are nearly impossible to meet, you

will be setting yourself up for failure. Then what? Stress! Set clear, realistic goals you can work toward and do your best to meet.

In what areas can you set goals? Any area! Scholastics, finances, fitness, career direction, school and community involvement, or spiritual goals, just to name a few.

You can set weekly, monthly, or yearly goals—whatever suits you—whatever keeps you striving for that goal. Lisa likes setting short goals. She says that short goals give her a greater chance of success. Plus every time she accomplishes a goal, it's a boost to her self-image.

Larry feels the same way. Short, obtainable goals make him feel better about himself. His increased confidence encourages him to set even greater goals.

Your goals don't have to be complicated. They can be simple, such as being nice to your brother or sister, showing up for class every day, finishing the book you started reading, or keeping your room clean. Well, to some teens these are complicated! Just don't think that your goals are irrelevant. If they matter to you, they are important and valid!

Also, set some long-term goals. Ask yourself what you want to be doing in one year, three years, five years, and ten years from now. Write your answers down and save them. You are not writing your future in cement, but you are giving yourself a direction.

Dear Jesus, I feel as if my life is going in ten different directions. I really want to know which direction you want me to go. Open my eyes so I'll see your leading. Amen.

Prime Time This Week

"Just follow the yellow brick road!" How nice for Glenda, the good witch, to direct Dorothy to her goal. Those little munchkins piped in, too! "Follow, follow, follow, follow, follow the yellow brick road!" Can't you just hear the tune in your head? Well, if only life were that simple. Jesus doesn't lay out the specifics of every person's life in the Bible, but the Bible *does* give us some general instructions, some goals to strive for. This week find out what some of them are, then follow!

Monday

Here's one of Jesus' top priorities for your life! Read Mark 16:15–18 and Matthew 28:18–20. Preach, teach, baptize, make disciples, and pray! Why are these things so important to the Lord? How can you start putting them into practice today? Pick a friend and tell him or her about Jesus today! _____

_____

_____

_____

Prime Prayer: Ask the Lord to help you realize that telling others about him is not just the job of ministers or fanatical Christians, but it's what he wants even *you* to do.

Tuesday

Your life is made up of activities and actions! Jesus has something specific to say about how he wants you to act toward others as you go through life! Read Luke

6:31–35. How can you put this into action? Are there some people you have been mistreating? Who? Write out a plan to start changing your actions. _____

_____

_____

_____

Prime Prayer: Ask the Lord to give you the maturity and strength to treat others lovingly, fairly, and kindly, just as you want to be treated.

Wednesday

Sex! Safe or not, God says, "no." Premarital sex is not part of his plan for your life! Read 1 Thessalonians 4:3. But God's Word is not just full of "do not's!" For a great list of "do's" in life, get comfortable and read Jesus' Sermon on the Mount in Matthew 5–7. List at least eight things the sermon instructs you to *do.* _____

_____

_____

_____

Prime Prayer: Ask Jesus to help you concentrate on all of the "do's" in the Bible so the "do not's" won't seem at all tempting!

Thursday

Read Matthew 6:10. Jesus instructs believers to pray for God's will to be done in their lives! That goes for you, too. Don't just wing it! Even Jesus prayed for his

Father's will to be done in his life, and he followed God's leading! Read about it in Luke 22:41–43. ____

_____

_____

_____

Prime Prayer: Pray for God's will to be done in your life each day, and that you will be able to accept his will and be obedient to it just as Jesus was.

Friday

What? Jesus wants you to pray? And he wants you to stay away from tempting situations? Read Luke 22:46. How can prayer keep you from giving in to tempting situations? _____

_____

_____

_____

Prime Prayer: Thank God today that prayer gives you the strength to stay away from things that are not pleasing to God!

This week's memory verse: Pick it! Write it! Remember it!

_____

_____

_____

_____

_____

Speak Up, Lord, I Can't Hear You!

I was crying to the Lord with my voice, and He answered me from His Holy Mountain.

Psalm 3:4 NASB

Sarah is frustrated. She prays and talks to God regularly, but her conversations seem one-sided. Is God really listening? Does he care about her troubles? Does he really give guidance? Is he still up there?

Hearing from heaven has fascinated people for years. It's especially discouraging to a teen who is making an honest effort at living a Christian life. Sarah will be happy to know that the problem isn't that God doesn't answer. It's that too often, we just can't seem to hear him. There's static on the line! Or perhaps we simply don't recognize God's solution (or don't want to admit that we know what he wants, because it's not what *we* want).

Psalm 3:4 tells us God *does* answer and respond when we talk to him. So, how can we hear him more clearly and recognize his answer? Here's how to clear the line:

1. *The Bible.* Many times the answer or encouragement you need is right in the Bible. As you read, a certain Scripture may suddenly have new meaning. It comes alive. It's just what you needed. That's God.

2. *Other People.* Often God will speak to you through something someone says. It catches your attention and applies to your situation. The person may have no idea he said something that helped you. But when someone shares from wisdom and experience, God uses it as an answer.

3. *Inner Listening.* After you pray, sit quietly and listen for the Lord to speak to you. This won't be an audible voice, but in the form of a thought in your mind, one that you know you didn't think up. If it's positive, good, loving, and in line with the Bible and God's nature, you can trust it. If it's evil or revengeful, it's not God.

4. *Change of Circumstances.* When something that was going wrong suddenly starts working out, or a new option is presented, some call it coincidence. Well, if it's something you've prayed about, I would call that God. He makes things happen that change our circumstances and answer our prayers.

5. *Follow after Peace.* Another way God can give you direction and answers is through his peace. In the Amplified Bible, Colossians 3:15 says to let God's peace be the umpire in your life. An umpire is the one who calls the shots and makes the final decisions. When you need an answer to a problem, see

which direction you feel peaceful going in. God leads through his peace.

Be on the lookout for the Lord, read your Bible, talk with other Christians, follow after peace, and listen for the Holy Spirit to speak. God does answer prayer. He does not pick and choose whose prayers he will answer. He answers all prayers in the way he sees fit. Trust his wisdom. He loves you. He will answer you. The more time you spend with him, the more easily you will recognize his voice.

Dear Father, remind me always that you hear when I pray, and that you answer in your own time, in your own way. I trust you. Amen.

Prime Time This Week

Every day this week, review and practice the five ways to hear from the Lord. Memorize them so that after you have prayed, you won't walk away and forget about them! Let's look at a few more things that can hinder or help your hot line to heaven.

Monday

In Psalm 5:1–3, David uncovers a great secret. First, he prays in the morning before his day gets into full swing. Then what does he say in verse 3? How does being expectant increase your chances of hearing God's voice? _____

_____

_____

_____

Prime Prayer: Pray that each day you will be looking for God's answer to your prayer, knowing he hears you and will respond.

Tuesday

Read Isaiah 59:2. How does unconfessed sin hinder hearing from God? What should you do? Right! Confess your sins to the Lord daily so your connection will be static-free! _____

_____

_____

_____

Prime Prayer: Ask God each day to forgive your sins of the day—list them individually—so your prayers won't be hindered.

Wednesday

What is the advice given in Psalm 46:10? How will this information help you tune in and listen for God?

_____

_____

_____

_____

Prime Prayer: Ask God to teach you how to be still before him, chasing all other thoughts away, so you can hear him speak to you.

Thursday

At the church in Antioch, Paul and fellow believers were gathered together. They were praising the Lord and fasting (skipping a meal for the purpose of prayer), and someone spoke to them. Read Acts 13:1–3. Who spoke to them? Praise put them in the proper mind-set to hear the Holy Spirit! List two ways you can praise the Lord during your prayer time. _____

_____

_____

_____

Prime Prayer: Pray to be a praiser because it opens up the way for the Holy Spirit to speak to you.

Friday

Do you have a tough decision to make? Have you ever prayed and then let peace help you make the decision? Read Isaiah 55:12. It confirms that God leads us through his peace. Close your eyes. Take a deep breath. Which option seems like the most peaceful answer to your dilemma? Go with it! _____

_____

_____

_____

Prime Prayer: Pray for God's peace to fill your heart so you know exactly what he wants you to do.

This week's memory verse: Pick it! Write it! Remember it!

_____

_____

_____

_____

_____

Tough Love

Beloved, let us love one another, for love is from God.

1 John 4:7 NIV

The wind howled, blowing the cold November rain hard against Julie's bedroom window. The windowpanes rattled. A bare oak limb scratched the side of the house, sending a chill up Julie's back. *What a lousy Saturday,* she thought. *I'm glad I'm driving to the mall. I'll pick up Mindy early and we can shop until the movie. Maybe we can see it twice.*

Julie pulled on her jeans and yanked a red turtle-necked sweater over her head.

"May I come in?" asked Julie's mother. "We need to talk a minute."

Oh boy, thought Julie. *Now what does she want?* "Sure, Mom. I'm just getting ready to leave."

"I know you wanted to drive the car to the mall, but the weather report says the storm's going to get worse. I don't want you to drive in—"

"Mom," interrupted Julie, "I'm a great driver. And you *said* I could use the car. You *promised!*" Julie jammed her fist deep into her jeans pockets.

"I'm sorry, honey. You can't use the car. I wouldn't even drive in this weather unless it was an emergency."

"This *is* an emergency," said Julie. She could feel her cheeks getting red. "Mindy's important to me. You just don't understand, Mom. Please! I promise to be careful."

"Julie, *you* just don't understand. I'm saying no because I love you." The door shut softly. Julie leaned her forehead against the cold window glass and stood for a long time watching the wet world rock in the wind. She sighed, then dialed Mindy's number.

"Mindy, this is Julie. I guess we can't go to the mall— because my mom won't let me use the car."

And because of love, whispered her heart.

> Lord, I know you are always loving me. But some- times I don't understand your love. The discipline and the restrictions are hard to accept, but I know they keep me safe and help me grow. Let me see your love in the difficult no's. Give me an understanding heart. Amen.

Prime Time This Week

Real love doesn't always mean sugar and spice, hugs and kisses. Just because your parents don't let you have your way doesn't mean they don't love you. They usu- ally have the wisdom to know what's best for you. Their discipline and guidance may be tough, but that's how love is sometimes! This week learn how to have more love for your family, why you are to love them, and what receiving your parents' tough love will bring you!

Monday

You can gain from all this! What will receiving your parents' tough, loving discipline bring you? Find out in Proverbs 13:1. Why does God call parents wise? _____

_____

_____

_____

Prime Prayer: Ask the Lord to make you accept your mom and dad's discipline, so you will grow wise.

Tuesday

Where do you get the love you need to love your family, especially when you don't *feel* like loving them? See 1 John 4:7–8. How will God's love help you love your family? _____

_____

_____

_____

Prime Prayer: Ask God to fill you with his love for your family.

Wednesday

You may think your family hasn't earned your love. Or, your parents get on your nerves and your brothers and sisters have been unkind. Okay, maybe you're right. But, that's not why you are to love them. What does John 13:34–35 tell you? _____

_____

_____

_____

Prime Prayer: Ask the Lord to help you love your family so others will know you love him.

Thursday

Is loving your family a one-way or two-way street? Read Matthew 7:12 to make sure you're on the right road. What does it tell you to do? _____

_____

_____

_____

Prime Prayer: Pray for the motivation to love others as you want to be loved.

Friday

Working on your relationship with your family is worth the effort. You'll find that friends come and go in life, but family is always around. How can you help make your family a pleasant place to be? If you can't think of anything, pray and quietly wait for the Lord to give you some suggestions! _____

_____

_____

_____

Prime Prayer: Ask the Lord to humble you and give you a servant attitude at home so your relationships there will be peaceful and loving.

This week's memory verse: Pick it! Write it! Remember it!

_____

_____

_____

_____

Splinters for Jesus

Don't copy the behavior and customs of this world, but be a new and different person with a fresh newness in all you do and think. Then you will learn from your own experiences how his ways will really satisfy you.

Romans 12:2 TLB

Have you ever stepped on some rough old wood or run your fingers up an aged boat paddle? How about a dry stick or a small wooden match? What happens nine times out of ten? You get a splinter! If you touch the object in the same direction of the wood's grain, no big deal. No splinter. It's going against the grain that forces a sharp, thin sliver of wood straight into your flesh. OUCH! Just the thought of it can send a chill up your spine!

Many times in our Christian life we have to go against the grain because it's what Jesus wants from us. If we drift along with the crowd to be popular or to fit in, doing things just because we think everyone else is (sometimes they're not), we won't get any splinters, but we also won't feel very close to God or very much joy on the inside.

Romans 12:2 beckons us not to blend in with the crowd and do what they're doing when we know it's wrong. The world is supposed to see a visible difference between Christians and non-Christians. Christians now have the ability and motivation to be new and changed people through the power of the Holy Spirit. When we go against the crowd we may lose a few so-called friends, get called a "goody-goody," or spend some Saturday nights at home with Mom and Dad. Those are splinters! Yet, doing these things for our Lord will teach us how following his ways will bring us true happiness. When you get a splinter for Jesus, his abundant love, like a big pair of tweezers, will quickly come to remove the splinter and the pain and replace it with his gentle touch.

Jesus, splinters hurt, but I know that I'm not really happy or doing your will when I mess up with my friends or in my thoughts toward others. Give me the courage to go against the grain for you. Amen.

Prime Time This Week

Standing out for Jesus has never been the way to win a popularity contest. Jesus himself knew it wouldn't be. He knew his followers would be made fun of and criticized for their dedication to him. It makes them stand out and be noticed because they are different. Christians are no longer the same. They've been changed on the inside. Jesus has made us new and fresh. Our behavior needs to reflect that change. Let's see how this week goes.

Monday

Accepting Jesus makes you a *new* person on the inside. Things are not the same, they're better. Read 2 Corinthians 5:17–20. What old things in your life need to pass away? What is an ambassador? How are you an ambassador for Jesus? _____

_____

_____

_____

Prime Prayer: Ask God for strength to get rid of old habits and ungodly actions so you can be a true representative of him.

Tuesday

As you get closer to Jesus, you realize there are things he doesn't want you to do, so you stop. But how will your friends react? Read 1 Peter 4:1–5. Who do they eventually have to answer to? Read 2 Corinthians 6:14 to see why you and your old friends don't mix any longer! Write the reason here. _____

_____

_____

_____

Prime Prayer: Ask God for courage as you step out of your old circle of friends and into a new one!

Wednesday

Do your non-Christian peers ever try to intimidate you because of your beliefs? Read 1 Peter 3:13–16. How can you keep from being accused of being a fake? What happens when you suffer for Jesus? _____

_____

_____

_____

Prime Prayer: Ask the Holy Spirit to keep you strong, yet gentle when you have to explain yourself to others and to keep your conscience clear. Don't give in. You'll be blessed.

Thursday

Can a person love the world and love the Lord at the same time? Read 1 John 2:15–17. What are the three things from the world, not from God? If we indulge in these things we make ourselves friends to the world. Check out James 4:4. How does friendship with the things of the world affect your relationship with God?

_____

_____

_____

_____

Prime Prayer: Ask God to teach you how to keep him as your first love and to help you desire only him.

Friday

Peer pressure gets tough. Jesus knows! He was pressured by Satan, but he never gave in. Finally what did the devil do? Read Matthew 4:1–11. _____

_____

_____

_____

Prime Prayer: Pray for persistence in resisting Satan so he'll finally give up! Start praising God and Satan will run!

This week's memory verse: Pick it! Write it! Remember it!

_____

_____

_____

_____

_____

Capture My Image

Then God said, "Let Us make man in Our image,
according to Our likeness."

Genesis 1:26 NASB

In a remote African village in Ethiopia, the native
people had never seen a Polaroid camera. They huddled
around the magical paper that had just appeared out of
the front of this new white man's contraption. Oohs
and aahs, laughter and amazement. They were
entranced by the photograph. A fuzzy-looking group of
young men was slowly coming into focus.

"Hey," shouted Benja, a young African shepherd boy.
"You have captured my image." Having only seen a
reflection of himself a few times before in a missionary's mirror, Benja recognized himself in the photo. His
image had been captured in the picture.

The word *image* means likeness. On the sixth day of
creation, God turned to his Son and said, "Let Us make
man in Our image." God had made heaven, earth, stars,
trees, birds, fish, and animals, but had not yet made
anything like himself. So he saved his most important

creation for last and created human beings in his own likeness. God wants us to be like him! The best way to be like someone is to imitate that person. The Bible even instructs us in Ephesians 5:1 to be imitators of our Lord.

Jesus lived his life on earth to be our example, someone we can imitate. We can be like Jesus through our attitudes and actions. He showed concern for the multitude who had not eaten by multiplying the bread and fish. He prayed for people with needs and healed them. Most important, he told them about the kingdom of God and how to spend eternity with his Father. Jesus was kind, compassionate, loving, and full of joy and peace. He didn't steal, lie, cheat, gossip, get drunk, tell off his parents, or step on others to push his way to the top!

We can imitate him in so many ways. God made us in his image. He intended us to be like him, to imitate the attitudes, characteristics, and actions of Jesus. He is our example. God wants us to capture his image.

> Dear Lord, you spent your life doing good and loving things for others. They really mattered to you. Help me to be more like you in what I say and do. Amen.

Prime Time This Week

Set aside a certain time this week to read through the four Gospels (Matthew, Mark, Luke, John). This will give you a clear picture of who Jesus is. Also, take a close look at the following examples that Jesus gives. All of them are things he did that you can imitate. As you put these principles into action, observe how you feel about yourself and how special you can make others feel. You *can* capture the Lord's image.

Monday

In John 4:5–10, Jesus gives us a clear example to follow. Why do we often overlook people who are less fortunate, less popular, or less appealing than ourselves? Is there someone at school or in your church who needs your friendship? Go ahead, speak up. _____

_____

_____

_____

Prime Prayer: Ask God to make you aware of the people others have pushed aside so you can be their friend.

Tuesday

Read John 13:3–17. What did washing the disciples' feet symbolize? Read 1 John 1:9. Jesus forgives us of our sins. Is there someone you need to forgive? Do it today.

_____

_____

_____

_____

Prime Prayer: Ask the Lord to give you a forgiving, servant attitude like the one he had when he washed the disciples' feet.

Wednesday

The prophecy in Isaiah 53:7–9 speaks clearly of the type of person Jesus was. He didn't talk back, insult others, gossip, swear, or tell nasty jokes. How can you follow him in this example? Why is it important to guard your words? _____

_____

_____

_____

Prime Prayer: Ask God to give you the willpower to only speak good things.

Thursday

Everywhere Jesus went he told people about the kingdom of God. Check out Luke 9:10–11. Challenge yourself this week to tell one person something the Lord has done for you. Who will it be? What will you say? _____

_____

_____

_____

Prime Prayer: Ask the Holy Spirit to give you the courage to tell others about God.

Friday

Jesus was a compassionate person. He understood how others felt and reached out to help them. Read Matthew 15:30–39. Choose three people to show compassion to this weekend. _____

_____

_____

_____

Prime Prayer: Ask Jesus to teach you to be compassionate and caring toward your family and friends.

This week's memory verse: Pick it! Write it! Remember it!

_____

_____

_____

_____

_____

Being a Winner!

Guest Author: Lenne Jo Crum

And the Winner Is . . .

> Do you not know that those who run in a race all run, but only one receives the prize? Run in such a way that you may win.
>
> 1 Corinthians 9:24 NASB

It is so exciting to win first place in something! In 1976 I won the America's Junior Miss title. I was ecstatic! The scholarships I received paid for my entire college education.

My reigning year was also the year our nation celebrated its two hundredth birthday. My schedule was extremely exhausting but very exciting. A speech with President Ford in front of Independence Hall on the Fourth of July, interviews on the "Tonight Show" and "Good Morning America." Plus, appearing in *Seventeen*, *Teen*, and *People* magazines. Wow, what a great year!

As my year as America's Junior Miss drew to a close, I had mixed emotions about giving up this honor of being a winner. However, I realized that I became a real winner, not when I won the crown, banner, and armful of roses, but years before when I had accepted Jesus into my heart as Lord of my life and believed the Bible was God's divine Word and love letter to his children.

The race God had set before me was learning to be faithful to him in all circumstances—with or without a "title." My eyes had to be focused on his glory, having Jesus as my finish line.

A true winner is someone who says yes to Jesus Christ. What kind of training does this race require? First, prepare for your race by warming up through prayer. Second, get a good workout by studying the Bible. The harder you train, the more skilled you will be as a runner.

Remember, God is only a prayer away. He is very much a gentleman and will not come barging into your life. Instead, he stands at the door and knocks. It is up to you to decide what to do next. Will you open the door of your heart to him? Be a winner by running his race!

On your mark . . . get set . . . go!

> Dear Jesus, please come into my heart and strengthen me for your race. Help me to see that beginning and finishing with you will make me a true winner. Keep me on course by fixing my eyes on you. Amen.

Prime Time This Week

All Christians are in a race. They are running toward their goal—Jesus Christ and eternal life with him. Paul tells us in this week's Scripture to run our race to win. Don't just hop along the racetrack. Get out there and run! This week you'll uncover some training tips from the handbook on life. These Scriptures will help you run with confidence, endurance, and joy.

Monday

First things first! Read 2 Timothy 2:5. If you want to win the prize, you have to compete according to the rules. Don't get disqualified! The Bible is your rule book. Make reading it a daily habit. You are off to a great start by reading this devotional book. Keep going! _____

_____

_____

_____

Prime Prayer: Ask Jesus to help you be more committed to reading your Bible so you'll know the rules for living your Christian life successfully.

Tuesday

Now that you're learning the rules, you'd better find out who it is you are running this race against. It's not other Christians. We're all on the same team! Who is your opponent, your adversary? Find out in Ephesians 6:12–13 and 1 Peter 5:8. Who is it? What are his goals?

_____

_____

_____

_____

Prime Prayer: Ask Jesus to keep you aware of your opponent so he won't be able to trip you up.

Wednesday

Any good athlete knows you never turn and look back to see how close the opponent is! Looking back will slow you down. What advice does Paul give in Philippians 3:12–14? Will God lead you to victory? Read 2 Corinthians 2:14. _____

_____

_____

_____

Prime Prayer: Ask Jesus to keep you looking forward— forgetting your past mistakes and moving on. When Satan tries to remind you of your wrongs, tell him to scram!

Thursday

A crooked path is harder to run than a straight one. What running tip does Proverbs 3:5–6 give to help you get the kinks out of your path? _____

_____

_____

_____

Prime Prayer: Ask God to help you trust him even when you don't understand the situation or why he's leading you in the direction he is. The result? A straight path.

Friday

Here are the secrets to running a good race. To begin, get rid of things that hold you back (bad influences, a lazy attitude), drop off the sin that keeps tripping you up, add patience to your run, fix your eyes and heart on your goal: Jesus Christ. Now, top it off with joy! Jesus' key to enduring his race was knowing the joy of the results. Read all about it in Hebrews 12:1–2. What is holding you back in your Christian life? What do you keep tripping over? What gets your eyes off Jesus? ___

_____

_____

_____

Prime Prayer: Ask God to give you the spiritual power to overcome the things that are messing up your race.

This week's memory verse: Pick it! Write it! Remember it!

_____

_____

_____

_____

_____

Moving Away

For I know the plans I have for you, says the Lord.
They are plans for good and not for evil, to give
you a future and a hope.

Jeremiah 29:11 TLB

"Dad, I'm not going! It's just not fair! What about my cheerleading? What about the Junior Miss Pageant? What about Manuel?" Jill's last words erupted in a moan of pain as she burst into tears and slammed out of the house. She had to tell Christi.

Christi, her best friend, had lived next door forever. They shared everything. Jill and Manuel and Christi and Rob had such fun together. They had plans! The spring prom, the county fair, picnics at the lake. Christi's aunt had a cabin there, and they knew where the key was. Jill's heart pounded at the thought of a day alone with Manuel.

"I have the worst news ever, Christi! You won't believe it. My dad's been transferred and we're *moving!* To Oakville, of all places. Oakville's the end of the world! What can I do?"

"Moving! What will *I* do?" Christi asked. "I'll die without you here. You're my best friend, Jill."

The friends huddled together on Christi's front step, arms around each other's shoulders. After a while Christi spoke.

"Jill, remember what Pastor Dave said on our ski trip? That God cares about every detail of our lives? That he's always here, waiting for us to turn to him with our problems? Why don't we pray!"

Jill bowed her head. "Lord, how can I ask you to stop Dad from being transferred? He's so excited about the new job. But please help me. You know how awful I feel about leaving here. If it's really your will, show me how to live through it."

"And Lord," Christi said, "don't let our friendship ever die. Amen."

The girls stood and walked toward the house. Jill brushed her sleeve across her wet cheeks. "Don't forget, Christi, we're definitely going to get an apartment together after graduation."

Thank You, Lord, that you are there to listen when we pray. Help me to remember that you will be there always, wherever I go, and that you are directing my life. Amen.

Prime Time This Week

It's really true! God's plans for you *are* for good, never bad. Our future with God is full of hope! Yes, God may change the direction of your life, working to get you on his plan. Not getting your own way may ruffle your feathers and upset you at first, but hang on! The reason is always for your good. God sees the big picture. He knows what's down the road for you. He knows when you start heading off in the wrong direction. Depending on your willingness, he has to twist and pull or gently nudge you in the best direction. This week you'll see the benefits of being putty in God's hand, allowing him to mold you and make you, direct you and design you according to his plan.

Monday

Didn't make the tennis team? Lost the school election? When life isn't going the way you want it to, it's time for some major trusting to take place! Read Proverbs 3:5–6. Who are you *not* to trust? Do you trust halfheartedly? What is the result of trusting God? _____

_____

_____

_____

Prime Prayer: Ask God to help you trust his divine wisdom in your life.

Tuesday

Paul's life was headed in the wrong direction. He was giving all the Christians a bad time, even getting them put in jail! That's when Jesus stepped in. Read Acts 9:1–19. How did God get Paul's attention? According to verse 15, what were God's new plans for Paul's life? What if Paul had said, "No way!" to God? _____

_____

_____

_____

Prime Prayer: Ask God to boldly step in when you're headed in the wrong direction. Now, be willing to follow his lead.

Wednesday

What happens when you resist God's plan for your life? You cause yourself a lot of turmoil! Just like Jonah! Read Jonah 1:1–17. Now read Jonah 2:1–10 to find out Jonah's plea to God. What happened to Jonah when he ran from God's plan? What happened when he followed it? _____

_____

_____

_____

Prime Prayer: Ask God to keep you accepting his plan for your life so you won't cause needless pain to yourself.

Thursday

When Jesus comes into your life, his plan is to change you for the better. He will give you new purpose, new direction, new meaning. Mary Magdalene is a perfect example. Read Luke 8:2. What was Mary like before Jesus? Then she became a follower of Christ, living for him. Read John 20:1–2, 11–18. Why do you think Jesus appeared to Mary first? _____

_____

_____

_____

Prime Prayer: Ask Jesus to cleanse you of your sins and help you follow his new life for you.

Friday

Jeremiah 29:11 tells us that God gives us hope. Hope is having a positive expectation that something will work out for the best. Hope keeps you motivated; it keeps dreams alive! What hope has God put in your heart? _____

_____

_____

_____

Prime Prayer: Pray that you will not give up the hopes in your heart, but that you'll learn to trust God's timing in making them happen!

This week's memory verse: Pick it! Write it! Remember it!

_____

_____

_____

_____

_____

Holy—To Be or Not to Be

Holy Holly

Try to stay out of all quarrels and seek to live a clean and holy life. . . .

Hebrews 12:14 TLB

Holly had just turned down another invitation to a hot party. Sometimes it just killed her on the inside. It was hard to say no because she liked being with her classmates. But Holly had made a commitment to Christ to be an example of him. She knew it was best to steer clear of situations that could be trouble. Saying no, however, wasn't the only tough thing for Holly. It was the way her friends had started to tease her. They couldn't quite understand Holly's new life-style. She was cute, well-liked, a class officer, and very musically talented. She also cared for others, always helping out wherever she could.

But Holly kept herself separated when she knew God wanted her to. For this the kids at school had nick-named her "Holy Holly." Normally when teens take a stand for Christ, they don't fit in with their old friends. They're different. They don't hang out, go to the wild parties, do drugs, and so on. As in Holly's situation, other students start talking behind their backs saying things like, "So, Holly thinks she's too good for us now," or, "She's on some religious kick. She'll get over it."

In reality, teens like Holly are only doing what God has asked. Holly *is* being holy. Holy simply means set apart from the rest of the world. People should see a visible difference in what *Christians* do and say.

Holiness also means to be morally pure. With God's help we are to be obedient to God's Word, making a constant effort to stay away from sin. Does that sound impossible in today's immoral and polluted world? That's why Hebrews 12:14 says to seek or pursue holiness. The word *pursue* means to keep going, keep striving. It is a process. If at first you don't succeed, try, try, again! That's exactly what Holly was doing. And if others want to tease her and call her Holy Holly, more power to her!

> Dear Lord, help me to choose in my heart to live a life that will be separated for you. Please keep me strong when my friends don't understand my stand. I love you. Amen.

Prime Time This Week

Several places in the Bible, God tells Christians to be holy because he is holy. To state it simply, God is asking us to be like him. That's a natural desire of a father. God *is* our heavenly Father. If we grow up like him, he'll be able to look at us proudly and say, "Yep, that's my girl." In response to that kind of love, you and I desire to please him, obey his Word, and to be holy. This week let's look at the idea of holiness and what it means in your teen years.

Monday

To be holy is to have the character of God. To be the kind of person God is, we are to be opposite of or separate from evil and worldliness. Read 2 Corinthians 6:14–18 and 1 Peter 2:9. How do these verses describe God's people? How are we different from others? ____

_____

_____

_____

Prime Prayer: Ask God to make you realize you are his— no longer in darkness, but in his light, made for the purpose of bringing his light to others.

Tuesday

The apostle Paul tells us what holiness is *not* to help us better understand what it *is*. Read 1 Thessalonians 4:3–7 (*sanctification* means "holiness"). Now see Colossians 3:5–10. List the characteristics given that are not holy. _____

_____

_____

_____

Prime Prayer: Ask God to help you remain pure in your thoughts and actions and ask him to forgive you for your wrongs in this area, if needed!

Wednesday

As you are pursuing holiness, you'll find it is humanly impossible to be 100 percent sin-free! That's one reason Jesus died for our sins—so we could have forgiveness and grace! Read about Paul's struggle with being holy in Romans 7:15—8:2. And when you do mess up, check out 1 John 1:9. Do you ever feel like Paul? Explain your battle to remain holy. _____

_____

_____

_____

Prime Prayer: Thank God right now for providing forgiveness through his son, Jesus, so you can keep striving to be holy.

Thursday

God wants us to be holy so we'll be like him. Yet there are more reasons. The holier or closer we are to God, the more useful we will be in his service. Read 2 Timothy 2:21. As you get closer to God, how do you think he might use you for his purposes? Now keep reading through verse 23. What four things does God want you to go after? _____

_____

_____

_____

Prime Prayer: Ask God to help you try to be a vessel for honor and service to him.

Friday

Joy, joy, joy! God's reason for wanting us to be holy isn't just so we'll please him and so the world will know we are different. It's also for us! Holiness, which is also obedience to God's Word, will fill you with joy and God's love. Read John 15:10–11. List an example of when you felt good because you knew you did the right thing. _____

_____

_____

_____

Prime Prayer: Pray that your heart will be filled with joy because you are living in God's love and doing what pleases him.

This week's memory verse: Pick it! Write it! Remember it!

_____

_____

_____

_____

_____

Sisterly Love

Handshakes and Hugs

And give each other a loving handshake when you meet.

1 Corinthians 16:20 TLB

The big tournament game is over, and your team won! The ol' blue and gold Tigers did it! They captured the state title. Everybody is so excited they just can't hold back. The players and the faithful fans are slapping high-fives, hugging with all their might, giving their hearty handshakes and firm back pats.

Having all witnessed the triumphant trophy-taking, the group was united together. They shared a special experience. And they couldn't help but reach out and touch!

The early Christian churches were the same way. They shared the unifying experience of seeing and knowing the Lord Jesus. Their lives were changed, they found new purpose, and they were excited. Like a winning team, they were bonded together with joy. In signing off several of his New Testament letters, the apostle Paul told the early Christians to greet one another with a warm, loving handshake or a holy kiss (cheek-style, I suppose). This sort of contact showed they were members of the same team, having a caring attitude. But there's more to this reach out and touch stuff!

A friendly handshake, a pat on the back, or a sincere hug is very comforting and encouraging. It can brighten your day and uplift your spirits. A caring touch says, "Hey, I'm on your side. Everything will be all right." Handshakes and hugs can chase away fear, loneliness, and tension, and they are good icebreakers!

The qualifications to be a handshaker or hugger are easy! All you need is a hand, a couple of arms, a willing heart, and someone to hug! Both you and the recipient will be encouraged. Plus, handshakes and hugs can be done anywhere—at church, at school, at the movies, at home. Don't be shy! Reach out and touch!

> Dear Lord, how easy it is to offer a hand or a hug to someone. Whether they need a hug or I do, please give me the courage so I can lighten their day and mine. Amen.

Prime Time This Week

Handshakes and hugs are just two ways to show caring with your hands. Because we see our hands constantly and use them for so many different things, we may take them for granted. But they are really very special and an absolute necessity in our lives. This week we are going to look at various ways the Bible tells us to put our hands to use.

Monday

The "Proverbs 31 woman" uses her hands in four specific ways. Read Proverbs 31:13, 19, 20, 31. For what purposes does she use her hands? How can you use your hands for the same useful purposes? Do you like to bake, sew, do crafts? _____

_____

_____

_____

Prime Prayer: Ask the Lord to encourage you to be productive and to put your hands to good use!

Tuesday

There are both positive and negative ways you can use your hands. Negative uses for hands would be punching, slapping, stealing, and making rude gestures. Positive uses would be a gentle touch, hugging, holding hands, a friendly wave, applause, and helping someone. Read Ephesians 4:28. What are the positive and negative uses listed in this verse?

_____

_____

_____

Prime Prayer: Pray to be a loving person who isn't afraid to pat a back or hug a friend in public.

Wednesday

It's okay to shake someone's hand when you meet them or greet them! Here's how to shake hands: Sincerely extend your hand to the other person. Grasp their hand firmly, but gently. Don't leave your hand like a "limp noodle" in theirs. A good handshake shows self-confidence and interest in the other person. Do you think a handshake or a high-five breaks the ice when you first meet someone? How does physical touch make people feel more at ease? _____

_____

_____

_____

Prime Prayer: Pray to remember to extend your hand to someone when you first meet them as if to say, "I'm happy to know you."

Thursday

Jesus is our role model for hand handling. He used his hands over and over for three specific purposes, all of them producing comfort in the lives of those he touched. Read Matthew 9:27–30. Here Jesus used hands to _____. Read Matthew 17:5–8. This time he used them to _____. Finally, read Matthew 19:13–15. Jesus used his hands to _____ for others. List three ways you could use your hands the same ways Jesus used his. _____

_____

_____

Prime Prayer: Ask Jesus to help you reach out and lay your hands on your hurting friends, to pray for them, asking him to heal them, or hold them to help chase away their fears.

Friday

To cleanse your hands means more than just giving them a good washing with soap and water. James talks about cleansing hands in this different way. Read James 4:8. Here the phrase, "Cleanse your hands," means to keep from sinning. It means not to participate in anything evil, filthy, or ungodly. What are four ways you could get your hands spiritually dirty? If you have "dirty" hands, use 1 John 1:9 to clean them up! _____

_____

_____

_____

Prime Prayer: Ask God to make you more aware of your hands so you can keep them spiritually clean by asking forgiveness for your sins.

This week's memory verse: Pick it! Write it! Remember it!

_____

_____

_____

_____

_____

A Heart Like Hannah's

For this boy I prayed, and the Lord has given me
my petition which I asked of Him.

1 Samuel 1:27 NASB

Hannah had dreamed since her childhood of grow-
ing up and becoming a mother. She fancied the idea of
cradling a helpless baby to her heart, feeling the tiny
creature nestled against her warm flesh. She longed to
feed it, nurture it, watch it grow. But as life often goes,
the dream of this young woman was not coming true.
For her womb was barren, her heart was aching, and
her arms were empty.

Hannah's husband Elkanah loved her desperately and
tried to comfort her. But Hannah could only cry and
she refused to eat. Hannah was sad. She wanted a child
and knew of nowhere else to turn than to the Lord her
God. So she retreated to the temple to pray. There she
poured her heart out to God. To him she made a brave
vow:

O Lord of heaven, if you will look down upon my sor-
row and answer my prayer and give me a son, then I

will give him back to you, and he'll be yours for his entire lifetime, and his hair shall never be cut.

1 Samuel 1:11 TLB

The Lord had mercy on Hannah and granted her plea. God blessed her with a son. She named him Samuel, which means "asked of the Lord."

Though it may have been hard for Hannah, when little Samuel was still a toddler, she took him to the temple priest, Eli, and gave Samuel up for the Lord's service. God kept his promise to Hannah. Hannah kept her promise to God. With a mix of joy and tears, Hannah returned home without Samuel. The Lord was so pleased with Hannah that he blessed her with five more children.

Samuel grew up as the Lord's helper, assisting the priest Eli, until he had matured. Samuel was chosen by God to be a prophet and was an important part of God's plan for the chosen people of Israel.

Hannah, like many of the women in the Bible, is an example of faith and courage for young women today. Her belief and trust in the living God is a model we can learn from.

The women of Bible times often lived with painful and challenging circumstances that caused them to rely directly on God and to remain faithful to him. As young women today, you can follow their godly example.

Dear God, I want to develop into a woman of faith and courage like the women in the Bible. Help me to study their stories and see their strength. Amen.

Prime Time This Week

Even though the women of Bible times were not perfect or sinless, God saw through their flaws and loved them. When they turned their hearts toward him, he accepted them and used them to his glory. This week you'll meet several of those women. They were ordinary people like you and me. They had ups and downs. But God chose to use them because of their faith in him. He'll do the same in your life and mine when we let him. Let's take a peek into the lives of Abigail, Ruth, Mary, Rahab, and Priscilla.

Monday

Meet Abigail. She was married to Nabal, a cruel and strange fellow who denied food to David, God's chosen leader. But Abigail knew David was the Lord's and she stepped in. Read 1 Samuel 25:1–42. How did Abigail's faith in God save David from sinning (vv. 32–33). How did Abigail honor God? What was her reward?

_____

_____

_____

Prime Prayer: Pray today for Abigail's courage to step in to help make God's plan happen in your life or someone else's.

Tuesday

Meet Ruth. Though Ruth was widowed at a young age, she promised to stay and care for her mother-in-law, also a widow, instead of seeking a new husband. Ruth was not a Jew but a Moabite woman. Because of her belief in God, she was honored and rewarded. Read the four short chapters in the Book of Ruth. What characteristics of Ruth's caught Boaz's attention (2:11–13; 3:10–11). In chapter 4, what was Ruth rewarded with?

_____

_____

_____

_____

Prime Prayer: Ask the Lord to teach you to honor your brothers and sisters in Christ and to be as kind and selfless as Ruth.

Wednesday

Meet Mary. As you know, Mary was chosen to be Jesus' mother. While she was still a virgin, engaged to Joseph, the angel Gabriel appeared to her with the big news. Read Luke 1:26–38. According to Mary's response to the angel's message in verse 38, why do you think God selected her? _____

_____

_____

_____

Prime Prayer: Ask the Lord to give you the courage to publicly declare yourself his servant and to be willing to accept his plan for your life.

Thursday

Meet Rahab. Rahab was not known around town for her high morals and sexual purity. She was not a Jew, but yet Rahab believed that the God of the Jews was the one and only true God. Therefore, God used her open heart to help carry out his plan. Read Joshua 2:1–22 and 6:1–25. What could have happened to Rahab if she had been caught hiding the spies? How did God honor her for honoring him? _____

_____

_____

_____

Prime Prayer: Ask God to grant you the belief, wisdom, and faith that Rahab showed.

Friday

Meet Priscilla (also called Prisca). Priscilla was a woman who knew the Lord and was dedicated to doing the work of the ministry and telling others about Jesus. She opened her home to the apostle Paul, and she and her husband Aquilla went on a missionary trip with Paul. Read Acts 18:1–3, 18, 25–26 and Romans 16:3–5. What were Priscilla's strong qualities? _____

_____

_____

_____

Prime Prayer: Ask Jesus to give you the confidence to share with others the truth about him and to open your home and heart to others.

This week's memory verse: Pick it! Write it! Remember it!

_____

_____

_____

_____

_____

About the Guest Authors

Lenne Jo Crum—Lenne Jo was America's Junior Miss in 1976. For her talent competition she recited an original poem entitled "Let Me." Lenne Jo is interested in creative writing and in teens. She is a Young Life leader and committee member. She is also involved in Bible Study Fellowship and has served as a Sunday school teacher. Lenne Jo has judged many pageants on the local, state, and national levels. She lives in Boise, Idaho, with her husband, Curtis, and two children, Gabriel and Whitney.

Judy Hyndman—Judy is a free-lance writer and a contributing writer for *Still Moments*. Judy is active in her church and her children's school activities. She enjoys baking, traveling, and photography. Judy lives in Los Olivos, California, with her husband, Ken, her son, Sean, and teenage daughter, Gwyneth.

Carolyn Johnson—Carolyn is the author of *Understanding Alcoholism* and *How to Blend a Family.* She has also written for *Virtue, Family Life Today,* and *Home Life* magazines. Carolyn is a free-lance writer. She enjoys traveling around the country visiting her blended family of nine grown children. Carolyn and her husband, Harry, live in Solvang, California.

Barbra Minar—Barbra is the author of *Lamper's Meadow* and *Unrealistic Expectations: Capturing the Thief of a*

Woman's Joy. Barbra has also written several children's books and articles for *Today's Christian Woman.* Barbra enjoys artwork and sharing a cup of tea with friends. She is the mother of three grown children. Barbra and her husband, Gary, live in Solvang, California.

Karen J. Sandvig—Karen is the author of *Falling into the Big L* and *You're What? Help and Hope for Pregnant Teens.* She has also created *Crying Out Loud* and other videos. Karen is the mother of two teenage sons. Karen, her husband, Doug, and the boys, Matt and Luke, live in Santa Ynez, California.

Has your study time challenged you and made you think about your life and important issues in a new way? Do you have some tough questions that need answers? Terrific! Asking questions shows you care. If you need help getting those questions answered, please write. My husband and I will do our best to help you out. We look forward to hearing from you!

Reverend Bill and Andrea Stephens
P. O. Box 3080
Covington, LA 70434